"*Wiser* is the wisest book ever written on how to use the wisdom of groups to make wiser decisions. Sunstein and Hastie are two of the most eminent social scientists of our era, and their wisdom shows through in this book. All managers need to know the insights they provide."

—**Max Bazerman**, professor, Harvard Business
School; author, *The Power of Noticing*

"Sunstein and Hastie have woven together the most cutting-edge research on behavioral economics and groups with real-world insights from Sunstein's experiences in the hurly-burly of the West Wing. *Wiser* will help leaders of organizations—whether they are the President of the United States or managers of small businesses—to reduce failures and make better decisions."

—**Nancy-Ann DeParle**, founding partner,
Consonance Capital Partners; former Assistant to
President Obama and Deputy Chief of Staff for Policy

WISER

Cass R. Sunstein
Reid Hastie

WISER

GETTING BEYOND
GROUPTHINK TO
MAKE GROUPS
SMARTER

HARVARD BUSINESS REVIEW PRESS

Boston, Massachusetts

Copyright 2015 Cass R. Sunstein and Reid Hastie
All rights reserved

Printed in the United States of America

10 9 8 7 6 5 4 3 2 1

No part of this publication may be reproduced, stored in or introduced into a retrieval
system, or transmitted, in any form, or by any means (electronic, mechanical, photocopying,
recording, or otherwise), without the prior permission of the publisher. Requests for
permission should be directed to permissions@hbsp.harvard.edu, or mailed to Permissions,
Harvard Business School Publishing, 60 Harvard Way, Boston, Massachusetts 02163.

The web addresses referenced in this book were live and correct at the time of the
book's publication but may be subject to change.

Library of Congress cataloging information forthcoming
ISBN: 978-1-4221-2299-0
eISBN: 978-1-62527-050-4

The paper used in this publication meets the requirements of the American National
Standard for Permanence of Paper for Publications and Documents in Libraries and
Archives Z39.48-1992.

Contents

Beyond Groupthink

Did you recently finish a project a lot later than you expected? You are subject to the planning fallacy, which means that you expect to complete tasks far more quickly than you do.

Are you confident that your friend will like that movie you recently loved? You might well be vulnerable to *egocentric bias*, thinking that if you like something, other people are going to like it too.

People tend to ignore the long term; to be unduly afraid of losses; to display unrealistic optimism; to make self-serving judgments ("what's fair is what's best for me!"); and to deal poorly with risks. For these reasons, and many others, each of us—as individuals—can get into a lot of trouble.

The last few decades have seen pathbreaking research on how people think, act, and sometimes blunder. Behavioral scientists have shown that human beings make all sorts of mistakes. By itself, this observation is not exactly news. What's important is in the details—the specification of what mistakes we make, and why.

Social scientists, most notably Daniel Kahneman in his masterful book on the topic, have distinguished between two ways of thinking: fast and slow.[1] Fast thinking, rooted in what behavioral scientists often call System 1, is rapid, automatic, emotional, and intuitive. Slow thinking, rooted in what is often called System 2, is slow, calculating, and deliberative. If we want to know what to do, especially in complex situations, System 1 is not reliable (even though it is good at escaping from trouble in a hurry). If System 2 is working well, slow thinking is an important safeguard, because it runs the numbers and usually comes up with the right solution. Unfortunately, System 1 is often in charge, and it is responsible for many of the errors that individuals make.

But what about groups? In this book, we begin with a simple question: *Do* groups usually correct individual mistakes? Our simple answer is that they do not. Far too often, groups actually amplify those mistakes. With respect to the planning fallacy, for example, groups turn out to be even worse than individuals are—which is a clue to a lot of failures in business, government, and daily life. Within groups, System 1 has a great deal of power.

We also ask a second question: *Can* groups correct individual mistakes? Our simple answer is that they can. We aim to explain how.

Sometimes groups get wiser with the help of some easy, informal methods or tactics. A simple tactic: group leaders often do best if they shut up and let other people speak. A slightly less simple method: managers are frequently more effective if they assign specific roles to group members, thus making it more likely that groups will get the information they need. Wise groups sometimes adopt "red teams" that are designed to identify vulnerabilities in existing practices or coming decisions.

You can also increase wisdom within a group or a firm by cultivating certain social norms that redefine what it means to be a team player—not to go along with the group, not to engage in happy talk, not to show unqualified enthusiasm for the boss's demonstrable brilliance, but *to add new information.*

Sometimes groups do best when they adopt more formal approaches. Groups can enlist modern technologies that provide astounding opportunities both to capture and to improve collective wisdom—through tournaments, prediction markets, and public comment processes. By the way, we didn't come up with the title of this book; it was produced by a collection of complete strangers, working on a website that we didn't know about until we decided to look for help with our title. We'll tell that tale in due course.

We also apply a central distinction from biology and modern computer science. The distinction can help people to improve group processes of all kinds by dividing decisions or problem-solving tasks into a creative, divergent-thinking stage and a critical, solution-integration stage. We will offer many specific suggestions to managers of all stripes, who are frequently faced with group processes that just aren't working, or aren't working well enough, and who want to know how things can be set right.

How Many Heads Are Better Than One?

Since the beginning of human history, people have made decisions in groups. In modern societies, they do so in companies, law firms, school boards, labor unions, religious organizations, governments, and international institutions. In all these cases and countless others, people assemble in groups, small or large, to decide what to do. As the saying goes, two heads are better than one, and if this is so, then three heads should be better than two, and four are better still, and with a hundred or a thousand, well, things are bound to go well. (We'll discuss some mathematical results that describe and constrain the power of group thought in chapter 8.) If group members really talk to one another, they can learn and make better choices, and the group can correct the mistakes made by some or many of its members.

This optimistic view has a long legacy. A prominent version can be traced directly to Aristotle, an early advocate of collective intelligence, who insisted that when people "all come together . . . they may surpass—collectively and as a body, although not individually—the quality of the few best . . . When there are many who contribute to the process of deliberation, each can bring his share of goodness and moral prudence; . . . some appreciate one part, some another, and all together appreciate all."[2]

Aristotle was alert to the possibility that group members, deliberating together, may add up what they know and disregard mistakes and thus improve on "the quality of the few best." The key point involves information aggregation, as different people appreciate different parts of a body of information and lead everyone to appreciate everything. We will spend a lot of time trying to figure out what Aristotle's claim might mean and how to make it become true.

In the twentieth century, the philosopher John Rawls spoke in similar terms: "The benefits from discussion lie in the fact that even representative legislators are limited in knowledge and the ability to reason. No one of them knows everything the others know, or can make all the same inferences that they can draw in concert. Discussion is a way of combining information and enlarging the range of arguments."[3] While Rawls's topic was democracy, his point extends to all groups, whether private or public, small or large.

But do groups actually succeed in surpassing the quality of the few best? Do they, in fact, combine information and enlarge the range of arguments? Do firms accomplish this feat? Do government officials? Unfortunately, the history of the human species suggests that all too often, groups fail to live up to their potential. On the contrary, many groups turn out to be foolish. They bet on products that are doomed to failure. They miss out on spectacular opportunities. They develop unsuccessful marketing strategies. Their investments and strategies go awry, hurting millions of people in the process.

Leaders of different stripes are sharply divided on the question of whether groups are likely to make good decisions. In business, many prominent leaders insist that you can't make good decisions unless you involve a lot of people, who provide safeguards against blunders. In government, some famously successful leaders, like President Franklin Delano Roosevelt, have tended to believe the same thing. Other, less successful presidents have isolated themselves and listened to a small group of like-minded advisers. In many circles, the conventional wisdom is that if you want a good decision, you have to talk to a ton of people.

On the other hand, we are all familiar with leaders who have great confidence in their own judgments and who believe that group judgments and most inputs from advisers tend to be a distraction and a waste of time. (Vladimir Putin is an example.) Many tyrants and some geniuses tend to think this way. Sometimes they succeed; some leaders, including tyrants, really are extraordinary and can think things through on their own. But far more often, they fail, partly because they do not and cannot know enough.

Their self-confidence is both delusional and extreme. But we should pause before entirely dismissing them. Making good group decisions can be hard, and the difficulty sometimes makes us wonder whether it is worth the effort. For some people, a good group discussion is a rare experience. Economists suggest that we should assess the value of decisions in terms of two considerations: the costs of decisions and the costs of errors. Group judgments increase the costs of decisions, because many people are involved. And such judgments can increase, rather than decrease, the number and the size of errors (and hence the error costs), if the group ends up making decisions worse.

This point brings us to *groupthink*. The idea, first elaborated by Irving Janis, suggests that groups may tend toward uniformity and censorship.[4] Janis was right: much of the time, both private and public groups blunder not in spite of group deliberation, but because of it. After deliberation, companies, labor unions, and religious organizations often make disastrous decisions. The same point holds for governments.

The term *groupthink* is memorable, and it has deservedly entered the popular lexicon. But many researchers have tried, with little success, to find evidence to support Janis's claims.[5] Janis believed that groups are especially likely to suffer from groupthink if they are cohesive, have highly directive leadership, and are insulated from experts. To support his account, he offered some arresting case studies.

But it is hazardous to draw conclusions from case studies that aren't exactly randomized controlled trials, and in any case, other case studies (involving the Nixon White House and the launch of the *Challenger* space shuttle) do not support Janis's claims. Experimental research fails consistently to link particular group characteristics, including those that Janis emphasized, to groupthink.[6] Janis's evocative account can be seen as akin to a work of literature rather than as a precise account of how groups go wrong or as helpful guidance for group success.

Janis also produced his theory before the rise of modern behavioral science, which has led to an independent literature— represented not only in Kahneman's *Thinking, Fast and Slow*, but also in Ariely's *Predictably Irrational*, Mullainathan and Shafir's *Scarcity*, and Thaler and Sunstein's *Nudge*.[7] To date, however, no one has focused, in any sustained way, on how the recent behavioral findings bear on the performance of firms and other groups. We aim to fill that gap. We want to bring behavioral research, including behavioral economics, in direct contact with the question of group performance.

In this way, we seek to go beyond the idea of groupthink to obtain a more precise understanding of the problem of group failures (including business and government failures involving teams and organizations) and to identify potential solutions. We elaborate on several decades of research, some of it our own, that helps to specify the mechanisms that account for the failures of various deliberating groups, and that points the way toward successful practices. Many of the most constructive ideas show the extraordinary value of small steps that can be implemented immediately and that have a big impact. Countless businesses can do better for their employees and their customers. The same is true for governments, and for many other groups, including charities, religious organizations, and educational institutions.

Sharing What We Know

The two of us have studied group decision making for many years, and this book draws heavily on our own empirical work as well as our experience.

From 2009 to 2012, one of us (Sunstein) served as administrator of the White House Office of Information and Regulatory Affairs (OIRA). OIRA helps to oversee federal rule-making in the areas of environmental protection, workplace safety, health care, immigration, agriculture, homeland security, and much more. In the federal government, as in so many other places, group decision making is the norm, and the fate of large projects and policies may depend on group dynamics.

The point of the OIRA process is to increase the likelihood that important rules and requirements will be consistent with law, will actually benefit the American people, and will not have unjustified costs. When the process works well, it is in part because different agencies of the federal government, all with their own information, are able to share what they know and thus to produce a better outcome. For example, the Council of Economic Advisers has specialists on economic effects. The Environmental Protection Agency (EPA) has experts on the environment. The US Trade Representative knows a great deal about trade implications. The Office of Science and Technology Policy has plenty of scientific expertise. When people from different offices and departments feel free to say what they know, group decisions get a lot better and big mistakes are avoided.

If, for example, the EPA is considering a rule that would reduce air pollution from power plants, it needs information from other people within the federal government. It needs to know about economics and science, and it might need to know about trade. True, the agency has its own specialists, but if it hears from other experts in those fields, it is likely to make much better decisions. As we will emphasize, the assignment of particular roles, ensuring that important perspectives are not ignored, is a hallmark of well-functioning groups. Careful cost-benefit analysis, a paradigmatic example of System 2 thinking, is also a crucial way of overcoming behavioral biases, including group biases.

Something similar can be said in the area of foreign policy. The idea of good process may sound boring, but when nations avoid foreign policy mistakes or make canny decisions, it is often because they have "good processes" in place to ensure that leaders learn what they need to know, and that valuable information is not missing or lost. Within the White House, the national security adviser has the job of running that process. If the person who serves in this role is dictatorial or proceeds without giving careful consideration to what a lot of people think, the process is unlikely to go well.

During the Bush administration, the judgment that Iraq had weapons of mass destruction was, in part, a failure of an entire process in which information was not properly sifted and aggregated. During the Obama administration, the decision to go after Osama Bin Laden was a gamble, but it was a good one, because National Security Adviser Thomas Donilon ran a masterful process and kept the president superbly informed.

Complacency, Anxiety, and Happy Talk

Good managers are acutely aware of the benefits of information aggregation, and they know that role assignment can reduce the risk of "happy talk." Happy talk occurs when group members say that all is going well and likely to go even better—that there is nothing to worry about. We think that happy talk is a pervasive source of group failures, and we will have a fair bit to say about why it is so harmful. In fact, happy talk is a principal target of this book.

In government, as elsewhere, role assignment may not be enough. We can divide the world of leaders into two kinds of people: the complacent and the anxious. Complacent leaders are relaxed, upbeat, and contented. They think that things are entirely under control. By contrast, anxious leaders are focused on possible disasters. They fear that things are about to go wrong and perhaps spiral out of control.

Complacent people are full of energy, excitement, enthusiasm, and optimism. They believe in their projects. Their enthusiasm is contagious. In the Obama administration, for example, most officials were not complacent, but some of them were; they thought that the Affordable Care Act could be implemented with only a few glitches, that Democrats and Republicans would work together, and that policies would work just as the administration hoped.

Complacent people tend to be immensely likable. They seem like perfect team players. They can tell a terrific story. Some of them are visionaries. They don't rock any boats. They are buoyant and full of smiles. They have plenty of ideas, many of which are excellent. They tend to be happy, and they like happy talk. It's tempting to hire and promote them. We won't name any names, but every presidential administration, like many other workplaces, has plenty of complacent, easygoing people.

By contrast, the anxious people may be optimistic, nice, even enthusiastic and full of smiles, but they are also troubled by concern, skepticism, and doubt. They believe in their projects and want them to work, but anxious people see obstacles, downsides, and challenges everywhere. Working with the Obama administration's complacent people, the anxious people would sometimes look doubtful, focused, negative, and occasionally severe. They would ask probing questions along the lines of, "What could go wrong? Did you think of this? Why haven't you planned for that?"

We will name two names. Nancy-Ann DeParle, who served as deputy chief of staff for policy from 2010 to 2012, is an exemplary anxious person. DeParle has had a lot of government experience. She is keenly well aware that competent, smart, and enthusiastic people can make big mistakes, especially if these people are not looking around the corner and thinking about worst-case scenarios. While she is immensely fair and one of the nicest people in the world, she is not always smiling. She has no problem looking people in the eye and doubting their plans, or telling them a firm no, in part because she is anything but complacent.

Here's a little story. When Sunstein was running OIRA, DeParle sent him a mildly anxious email late one night, asking, "How's the regulation coming?" Sunstein had no idea which regulation she meant. He responded, "I don't know which regulation you have in mind, but most of them are coming pretty well, so chances are that this one is coming well too." DeParle replied briefly: "hug."

Sunstein was a bit amazed, and also touched, because nice as DeParle is, she isn't prone to sending hugs. Sunstein answered, "That's the nicest email of the year." DeParle promptly wrote back to explain that she had written "ghg," for "greenhouse gas," and her cell phone had autocorrected to "hug." (Oh well.)

DeParle isn't a hugger. She doesn't like happy talk. She makes everyone around her, and everyone below or above her, much wiser, although sometimes also a bit uncomfortable. You can't rerun history, but there's an argument that if she had continued to serve in the Obama administration, the troubled rollout of HealthCare.gov in 2013 would have been executed better and the website would have worked. Whether or not that is so, anxiety concentrates the mind, and an anxious leader concentrates a lot of minds. Anxiety, like most emotions, is contagious—which is an important lesson for managers to keep in mind.

In President Obama's first term, Jeff Zients served as deputy director for management and later as acting director of the Office of Management and Budget. He is upbeat, funny, and unfailingly genial, and his brow is seldom furrowed. Everyone loves Zients, but he's fully capable of productive anxiety, especially when the stakes are high. In the private sector, he was known as a superstar manager. During the 2013 fiasco that was the early days of Health-Care.gov, President Obama made a really smart move in asking Zients to fix the problem—as Zients did. The president also made a smart move in asking Zients to return to the White House as director of the National Economic Council.

Good managers have to be anxious, even as they must inspire loyalty and affection in their colleagues and subordinates, and Zients has an extraordinary ability to combine anxiety, likability, and competence. Some of his colleagues have referred to him as "the quarterback," not only because he has a terrific throwing arm, but also because his leadership ability is manifested in insights and performance, not happy talk.

Anxious people like DeParle and Zients are indispensable in business and government, because they cut through, and overcome, the risk of groupthink. They work a bit like devil's advocates (discussed in chapter 6), but they're a lot better, because everyone knows that they mean business and aren't playing any kind of game. They say what they think. Even better, they say what they fear. With their very different styles, they keep asking, "What can go wrong?"

When groups ultimately do well, it is often because they have anxious leaders and hence are better able to obtain and aggregate dispersed information—and to ensure that the groups know everything that their members know. Groups are also capable of learning, because anxiety is a great motivator. Groups need a little anxiety, maybe even a lot of it. They need a culture that enables them to find out what they need to know.

Realism, Optimism, and the Path to Wiser Groups

The good news is that if discussion is properly structured and if groups adopt the right norms and practices, they can create that culture. The bad news is that in the real world, discussion often leads people in the wrong directions. Many groups fail to correct the mistakes of their members. On the contrary, groups often amplify those mistakes. If group members are unrealistically optimistic, groups may be more unrealistic still. If people within a firm are paying too little attention to the long term, the firm will probably suffer from a horrible case of myopia. There is no evidence that the judgment mistakes uncovered by behavioral scientists are corrected as a result of group discussion.

Many of the most serious blunders made by companies, public officials, and religious organizations are a direct result of the problems that we will trace here. When companies launch products that no one wants to buy, it is often because the doubters have tried to be team players and silenced themselves. When officials propose environmental rules that are too weak, too draconian, or simply misdirected, it is often because group discussion has failed.

As we will see, wise groups and their managers are fully alert to the risks of suboptimal group processes and take concrete steps to counteract them. With the rise of the internet, there are unprecedented opportunities to take such steps. Groups can pool the information that their members have. They can also reach outside themselves to draw on the dispersed knowledge of hundreds, thousands, or even millions of other people.

Drawing on empirical research, we identify a number of concrete solutions for making groups wiser. Some of those solutions are straightforward; for managers, the steps require leadership, determination, understanding, and a little creativity. Other solutions call for the use of modern technologies and may require some investment in both time and resources. Some of the solutions are informal and can be instituted overnight; others require at least a degree of formality and call for advance planning. Different approaches will work for different groups.

One of this book's recurring themes is that one size does not fit all. But if groups and their leaders have a fuller understanding of how things go wrong, they will be in a much better position to make things go right.

The Plan

This book is divided into two parts. Part 1 explores the sources of group failure. Chapter 1 establishes the context, describing why we deliberate and discuss problems in groups, what our hopes are when we do so, and the challenges that groups face. The principal focus is on how groups may fail to obtain important information— and on how their leaders and members tell dissenters, or people who have a different perspective, to shut up.

Chapters 2 through 5 explore four causes of group failure. First, groups do not merely fail to correct the errors of their members; they can amplify these errors. Second, groups fall into herds, as group members follow the statements and actions of those who speak or act first, even if those statements and actions lead the group in unfortunate, terrible, or tragic directions. Third, groups tend to get more extreme—as, for example, when a group of people inclined to suffer from excessive optimism becomes still more optimistic as a result of internal discussions. Fourth, members emphasize shared information at the expense of unshared information and thus do not give the group the benefit of critical and perhaps disturbing information that one or a few people have.

Part 2 turns to sources of group success. Chapter 6 begins with an account of seven methods, most of them quite simple, that can be used to reduce the risk of failure. Each method is designed to counteract the four failures that we identified in part 1. Our focus is on group deliberation and how to make it better. We emphasize the importance of self-silencing leaders and the value of role assignment, implicit or explicit.

Chapter 7 details the immense importance of distinguishing between two very different processes: (1) the identification of a list of potential solutions and (2) the selection of the preferred solution. In identifying a list of potential solutions, groups must be flexible, imaginative, and even a bit sloppy to open things up. In selecting an actual solution, it is important for groups to be tight and analytic—to close things down. Many groups do poorly because they mix up the two kinds of inquiries and, in particular, because they close things down at the very stage where they should be opening up to produce a list of potential solutions. We draw out this distinction in detail in chapter 7, but it is helpful to keep it in mind throughout the book.

In chapter 8, we explore the purported wisdom of crowds. The idea amounts to a celebration of the occasionally amazing performance of *statistical groups*, that is, groups whose members do not deliberate with one another at all but who answer a question or solve a problem independently. We show that crowd wisdom comes from some simple arithmetic—and that the same arithmetic explains why crowds can also be unwise. In some circumstances, statistical groups do poorly, and we spell out what those circumstances are. For groups, and especially firms, it is a mistake to assume that crowds are always wise. It is much better to understand why and when crowds turn out to be wise, and to build on that understanding to improve group deliberation. A central point here involves the importance of diversity and dissent.

In chapter 9, we discuss the role of experts. We show that it is often a big mistake to chase the expert. If you want to get the right answer, you'll do better to consult a bunch of experts, rather than looking for the one who seems best.

In chapters 10, 11, and 12, we explore new and more creative methods, often enlisting the internet to obtain ideas. For example, both the private and the public sectors are making innovative use of tournaments, by which large populations can be asked to submit their ideas. Even if the prize is relatively small, this approach can produce pathbreaking innovations. Chapter 10 shows how.

In chapter 11, we turn to prediction markets, which invite people to put their money on the line, saying, for example, whether a product or a movie will do well, whether the weather will get lousy, or whether a leader will lose his or her job. As we will see, prediction markets have proved stunningly accurate. Chapter 12 describes how groups can learn a lot from seeking public comment.

In chapter 13, we encounter the mysterious Factor C, a collective-intelligence factor that suggests that certain personality characteristics—above all, social sensitivity—can make groups perform better. Wise groups rely on a combination of incentives and architecture, but they also benefit from certain personalities, which they can also cultivate and help to produce. Some personal characteristics are innate, but others can be learned. Basketball's all-time best player, Michael Jordan (sorry, LeBron), was a great learner. With respect to Factor C, he got a lot better. Groups are unlikely to have anyone like Michael Jordan, but they do far better when they promote learning of multiple kinds.

PART 1

How Groups Fail

1

From High Hopes to Fiascos

When managers and other leaders are deciding how to proceed, they usually talk the problem through. But why, exactly, is it helpful to talk the problem through? Why and when is deliberation important or even desirable?

A big part of the answer must be that if people talk to one another, they will end up with wiser judgments and better outcomes. But does deliberation actually have this effect? This is a crucial question, and an empirical one, which cannot be answered by intuition or anecdotes. By imposing pressure on one another, group members may reach a consensus on falsehood rather than truth. A group of like-minded people, prone to error and with similar inclinations, is particularly vulnerable to this problem. If a bunch of people think that a complex government program is going to work immediately or that an untested, new product will be a big hit, we might have a bad case of happy talk.

To explain why groups go wrong when they deliberate, we investigate two types of influences on group members. The first type involves *informational signals*, which lead people to fail to disclose what they know out of respect for the information publicly announced by others. In the federal government, for example, people might silence themselves because they think that an official who does not share their views and who has his own information must be right. If the secretary of defense has a strong conviction about whether military intervention is a good idea, the people who work for the secretary might shut up, not because they agree, but because they think that the secretary probably knows what he is doing.

In the private and public sectors, leaders often seem to have a halo, which makes them appear unusually sharp and smart. Their jokes are funnier, their wisdom is wiser, their perspective wider, their questions more probing. In government, Sunstein noticed exactly this phenomenon, with civil servants occasionally treating his own tentative and insufficiently informed judgments as if they were far cleverer than they actually were. The halo can be fun to experience, especially if you have an ego, but it is also a real problem. It encourages happy talk and makes the group more likely to err. Anxious employees provide an important corrective, because they are willing to wonder whether the leaders are right. And if the leaders themselves are anxious—if they have a smile and personal warmth but also a troubled little voice in their heads asking, *What am I missing here?*—they will make their groups better.

The second type of influences involves *social pressures*, which lead people to silence themselves to avoid various penalties. In many cases, what matters is the mere disapproval of others, but if those others are important, the disapproval could lead to serious personal risks. Within firms, people often stay quiet and decline to disclose what they know, not because what they know is unimportant, but because they do not want to seem foolish or disagreeable. They are especially unlikely to speak up if the leaders or most others in the group seem to have a clear conviction. Is it really worthwhile to make the boss sad or mad?

From the boss's point of view, the answer should be yes, because the boss might learn something. But some bosses don't see things that way, and many employees know that it might well be better just to shut up. Here again, the right kind of anxiety can go a long way, because anxious employees will not worry much about social pressures and because anxious bosses welcome a wide range of views.

As a result of these two types of influences, groups run into four independent problems:

- Groups do not merely fail to correct the errors of their members; they actually *amplify* those errors.

- Groups fall victim to *cascade effects*, as group members follow the statements and actions of those who spoke or acted first, even if those statements and actions lead the group in unfortunate, terrible, or tragic directions.

- Groups become more *polarized*, ending up in more extreme positions in line with the predeliberation tendencies of their members—such as when a group of people, inclined toward excessive optimism, becomes still more optimistic as a result of internal discussions.

- Groups focus on shared information—*what everybody knows already*—at the expense of unshared information and thus fail to obtain the benefit of critical and perhaps troubling information that one or a few people have.

Because of these problems, groups often fail to achieve their minimal goals of correcting individual mistakes and aggregating the information actually held by their members. A confident, cohesive, but error-prone group is nothing to celebrate. On the contrary, it might be extremely dangerous both to itself and to others. A promising start-up may fail as a result. A government agency might waste taxpayer money; a new federal program might fail. A large business may continue on a badly mistaken course, even though it should have pulled the plug long ago. A law firm might press a doomed litigation strategy. When groups make poor or self-destructive decisions, one of these four problems is usually the explanation.

Positive Prospects

All over the world, deliberating groups start with high hopes. They're especially likely to be hopeful if each member thinks well of the others—if people are friendly, respectful, and engaged with one another socially as well as professionally. And while we will spend a lot of time showing why optimism about group decisions is often wrong, it is sometimes right. If deliberating groups do well, we can imagine three principal reasons.

1. *Groups are equivalent to their best members.* One or more group members might know the right answer, and other members might become convinced that this answer is right and therefore accept it. If group members are listening, the group will perform at the level of its best members. If many or at least some members suffer from ignorance or from a form of bias that leads to error, others should correct them. Deliberation can fix individual errors rather than propagate them in a way that allows the group to converge on the judgment of its wisest or most accurate member.

Imagine, for example, that fifteen people are trying to make some prediction about the likely fate of some product, and that one of the fifteen is both an expert and a superb prognosticator. Maybe the other group members will quickly see that they have an expert in their midst, and they will follow this person's lead. Consider "eureka" problems, in which the right answer, once announced, is clear to all. A trivial example: Why are manhole covers round? Answer: Because if they were almost any other shape, a loose cover could shift orientation and fall through the hole, potentially causing damage and injuries. (Of course!)

There are less trivial cases, requiring clever solutions to seemingly intractable problems, where the solution, once announced, is immediately clear to all. For such problems, groups should be expected to agree on the answer as announced by the member who actually knows it. Someone may know, for example, that a new tablet or cell phone has a fatal (but subtle) flaw, or that a website just isn't ready for prime time, or that a military strike is unlikely to have its intended effect.

2. *The whole is the sum of the parts: aggregating information.* As Aristotle suggested, deliberation could help people to share existing information in a way that leads the group as a whole to know more

than any individual member does. Suppose that the group contains no true experts on every aspect of a question, but that helpful information is dispersed among the members so that the group is potentially expert even if its members, considered individually, are not. Well-functioning companies often create cross-functional teams to aggregate information in just this way. If everyone is working together and listening to one another, the organization will be able to aggregate information to get a full picture of, for example, the effects of a proposed rule designed to reduce air pollution from power plants.

Or suppose that the group contains a number of experts, but that each member is puzzled about how to solve a particular problem. Deliberation might elicit the relevant information and allow the group to make a sensible judgment. In this process, the whole is equal to the sum of the parts, and the sum of the parts is exactly what is sought. No member can have all the parts.

When a group is trying to solve a crossword puzzle, something of this kind often occurs, as different group members contribute what they know. Many problems are like crossword puzzles in the sense that small groups do better than individuals, and large groups do better than small ones—simply because each person knows something that others do not, and it is easy to share and combine the dispersed information. As we will see, social media and prediction markets often do well for similar reasons.

3. *The whole goes beyond the sum of the parts: synergy.* The give-and-take of group discussion might sift information and perspectives in a way that leads the group to discover an innovative solution to a problem—a solution in which the whole is actually more than the sum of its parts. In such cases, deliberation is a powerful form of information aggregation, through which

the exchange of views leads to a creative answer or solution. If a group is seeking to improve the design of an automobile, a tennis racquet, a tablet, or a cell phone—or to come up with the right response to a threat to national security—the exchange of ideas can produce creative solutions that go far beyond any simple aggregation of what group members thought before they started to talk. The same is true if people are trying to write a play together or to come up with a sensible policy to deal with the problem of childhood obesity. And in fact, groups can be highly innovative, especially if divergent thinking is nurtured and minority views are welcome.

Confident and Unified

To what extent do these three mechanisms work in practice? Two points are entirely clear.

First, group members tend to become far more confident of their judgments after they speak with one another.[1] A major effect of group interactions is a greater sense that the postdeliberation conclusion is correct—whether it actually is or not. One reason is that corroboration by others increases people's confidence in their judgments.[2] If your colleagues or friends tell you that you are right, you are more likely to think that you are right, even if you are pretty confused (and wrong).

Confidence is certainly a good thing, but as we will see, it is not so good if people end up being both confident and wrong. A great risk of group deliberation is that it will simultaneously produce great confidence and grave error. Leaders are particularly likely to get in trouble for this reason. Group members tend to like to please their leaders, who will therefore not tell the group what it needs to know.

Second, deliberation usually reduces variance. After talking together, group members tend to come into accord with one another. Before deliberation, group members are often far apart; that is one reason that deliberation seems important or necessary. After deliberation, they tend to come into agreement (especially but not only if they are close-knit or have frequent interactions). It follows that members of deliberating groups will converge on a position on which members have a great deal of confidence. We will soon see some examples of this phenomenon in Colorado, where discussion led both liberals and conservatives to end up unified on major political questions, but with a wider chasm of disagreement between the two groups after discussion.

Convergence on a particular position is fine, of course, if that position is also likely to be correct. But if it is not, then group members will end up sharing a view in which they firmly believe, but which turns out to be wrong. Most of us are familiar with situations in which groups are confident, unified, but mistaken. The Bush administration's belief that Saddam Hussein had weapons of mass destruction is one example. The Obama administration's unwarranted confidence in the initially disastrous HealthCare.gov website, prelaunch, is another.

Truth versus Majority Rule

Unfortunately, there is no good evidence that deliberating groups will consistently succeed in aggregating the information held by their members. The basic lesson is that people pay a lot of attention to what other group members say and do—and that they do not end up converging on the truth. In fact, they often ignore their own beliefs and say that they believe what other people believe.

There is a clear warning here about the potential effects of not only group deliberation but also social media, which can lead people to accept falsehoods.[3]

Consider this example from recent research. Suppose that people are provided with the following statement: "Oatmeal contains soluble fiber, which reduces your low-density lipoprotein (LDL), the 'bad' cholesterol." (As it happens, this statement is true.) If people are informed of the true-false rating by "a majority of others like you" (on a scale of 1 to 6, from "definitely false" to "definitely true"), they are much influenced by the crowd. Not surprisingly, people tend to go along with the crowd if they tend to think independently that the crowd is right. Also not so surprisingly, people tend to go along with the crowd if they believe that the answer is unclear and debatable.

But strikingly, people also tend to go along with the crowd if the answer is false, even if they have independent reason to believe that it is false. The authors conclude that people's answers come close to supporting the hypothesis that "people always follow the collective credibility rating, even when they are sure that the statement is true or false."[4] Here is a major warning for managers who might find that their employees agree on some course of action, *not* because they have reason to think that it is right, but because they think that most other people think that it is right.

A classic study demonstrates that majority pressures can be powerful even for factual questions to which some people know the right answers.[5] The study involved twelve hundred people, forming groups of six, five, and four members. Individuals were asked true-false questions involving art, poetry, public opinion, geography, economics, and politics. They were then asked to assemble into groups that discussed the questions and produced answers.

The views of the majority played a dominant role in determining each group's answers; people tended to go along with what most people thought.

The truth played a role, too, but a lesser one. If a majority of individuals in the group gave the right answer, the group's decision moved toward the majority in 79 percent of the cases. If a majority of individuals in the group gave the wrong answer, the group's decision nonetheless moved toward the majority in 56 percent of the cases.

The truth did have an influence—79 percent is higher than 56 percent—but the majority's judgment was the dominant one. And because the majority was influential even when wrong, the average group decision was right only slightly more often than the average individual decision (66 percent versus 62 percent). What is most important is that groups did not perform nearly as well as they would have if they had properly aggregated the information that group members had.

Other studies find that with respect to questions that have definite answers, deliberating groups tend to do about as well as or slightly better than their *average* members—but not as well as their *best* members.[6] (So much for Aristotle.) So group members usually do *not* end up deferring to their internal specialists. Often truth does not win out, even if someone in the group knows what is true.

The most that can be said is that groups will often converge on the truth if (1) the truth begins with at least some initial support within the group and (2) the task has a demonstrably correct answer.[7] The second condition is especially hard to fulfill. In business and in government, many groups have to make predictions: Will a new employee perform well? Who should be promoted? Will a product sell? Will an environmental regulation save a lot of lives? Alas, in such cases, no answer may be demonstrably correct. When a group outperforms most of its individual members, it often does so because the issue is one for which a particular answer can be demonstrated, to the satisfaction of all or most, to be right. Even in that situation, which is not so usual, the group might not do well if the demonstrably correct solution lacks much support at the outset.

A good way to predict a judgment of a group is to ask: *What did the majority think, before people started to talk?* For optimists about group judgments, that's unfortunate. More specifically, and depending on the task, the central tendency of group members before they start to talk provides a pretty good forecast of how the group as a whole will end up. It follows that if the majority is wrong, the group will usually be wrong as well. With groups of experts, the same conclusion holds.

In fact, group discussion may turn out to be less helpful than a simple effort to elicit people's independent views. In the words of Scott Armstrong, an expert on forecasting at the Wharton School, a "structured approach for combining independent forecasts is invariably more accurate" than "traditional group meetings," which do "not use information efficiently."[8] Those are strong words, but there's a lot of truth in them. Let's now turn to this claim.

Statistical Groups versus Deliberating Groups

A great deal of evidence suggests that under certain conditions, a promising way to answer factual questions is this: put the question to a large number of people, and take the average answer. As emphasized by James Surowiecki in his engaging and illuminating book, *The Wisdom of Crowds*, the average answer, which we might describe as the answer of a statistical group, is often accurate, where accuracy is measured by reference to objective facts.[9]

Many of the studies of statistical groups involve quantitative estimates, and the studies seem to show a kind of magic, potentially used by businesses and governments hoping to work some magic of their own. Consider a few examples:

- In an early study, Hazel Knight asked college students to estimate the temperature of a classroom.[10] Individual judgments ranged from 60 degrees to 85 degrees; the statistical judgment of the group was 72.4 degrees, very close to the actual temperature of 72 degrees. That estimate was better than 80 percent of the individual judgments.

- When people are judging the number of beans in a jar, the group average is almost always better than the judgments of the vast majority of individual members. In one such experiment, a group of fifty-six students was asked about a jar containing 850 beans; the group estimate was 871, more accurate than that of all but one of the students.[11]

- The British scientist Francis Galton sought to draw lessons about collective intelligence by examining a competition in which contestants attempted to judge the weight of a fat ox at a regional fair in England. The ox weighed 1,198 pounds; the average estimate, from the 787 contestants, was 1,197 pounds, more accurate than any individual's guess.[12]

In light of these findings, many groups might want to answer questions not through deliberation, but simply by consulting people and selecting the average response. Imagine that a large company is attempting to project its sales for certain products in the following year; maybe the company needs an accurate projection to know how much to spend on labor and promotion. Might it do best to poll its salespeople and trust the average number? Armstrong suggests that the answer is often yes.[13] Or suppose that a company is deciding whether to hire a new employee. Should it rely not on deliberation, but on the average view of its relevant personnel?

In part 2, we will return to these questions and recommend some methods that can improve on simple arithmetic averaging (prediction markets and the Delphi method). For now, let us simply note that statistical groups often do better than deliberating groups, because the former rigorously incorporate all the information that their members have.

Two Sources of Self-Silencing

There are two reasons why exposure to the views of others might lead people *not* to disclose or act on what they know.

Informational Signals

The first reason people might stay silent involves the information conveyed by what other people say and do. Suppose that most people in your group believe that some proposition is true. If so, you have reason to believe that the proposition is in fact true, and this reason might seem to outweigh your purely private reasons to believe that the proposition is false. Sensibly enough, you might disregard your own information if most group members disagree with where you are headed. The informational signal from the group is strong enough to trump your personal one.

It is in part for this reason that whenever group members are isolated or in the minority, they might not speak out. They might simply defer to the informational signal provided by the statements or actions of others. In a law firm, for example, most group members might be quite optimistic about their likely success in court. (We have noted that human beings have a pervasive tendency toward unrealistic optimism.) Their optimism might lead the firm's skeptics to silence themselves on the ground that their own judgments must be ill informed or wrong. The problem is that if the skeptics refrain from speaking out, the group could lose important information—and depending on the context, the consequences could be serious or even catastrophic.

A famous and revealing example is the failed American invasion of Cuba at the Bay of Pigs. The invasion, designed to overthrow the revolutionary Cuban government headed by Fidel Castro, failed because President Kennedy's advisers said nothing, even when they had reason to believe that the mission would not succeed. In the event, two American supply ships were sunk by Cuban planes, two ships fled, and four did not arrive in time. The Cuban army, consisting of twenty thousand well-trained soldiers, killed a number of the invaders and captured most of the remaining twelve hundred. The United States was able to obtain release of the prisoners, but only in return for $53 million in foreign aid to Cuba, alongside international opprobrium and a strengthening of relations between Cuba and the Soviet Union.

Soon after the failure, President Kennedy asked, "How could I have been so stupid to let them go ahead?"[14] Kennedy's advisers were an exceptionally experienced and talented group. Notwithstanding their experience and talent, no member of that group opposed the invasion or proposed alternatives. Some of Kennedy's advisers entertained private doubts, but they "never pressed, partly out of a fear of being labeled 'soft' or undaring in the eyes of their colleagues."[15]

The failure to press those doubts mattered. According to Arthur Schlesinger Jr., a participant in those meetings, Kennedy's "senior officials . . . were unanimous for going ahead . . . Had one senior advisor opposed the adventure, I believe that Kennedy would have canceled it. No one spoke against it."[16] Schlesinger suppressed his own doubts but did not object: "In the months after the Bay of Pigs I bitterly reproached myself for having kept so silent during those crucial discussions . . . I can only explain my failure to do more than raise a few timid questions by reporting that one's impulse to blow the whistle on this nonsense was simply undone by the circumstances of the discussion."[17]

As the Bay of Pigs example suggests, the strength of the informational signal will depend on how many people are giving it, and on how admired, intimidating, or powerful they are. If the group contains one or more people who are known to be authorities or who otherwise command a lot of respect, then other group members are likely to silence themselves out of deference to the perceived or real authority. Moreover, people do not like being sole dissenters. If all but one person in a deliberating group have said that some proposition is true, then the remaining member might well agree that that proposition is true, even to the point of ignoring the evidence of his or her own senses.

The psychologist Solomon Asch memorably established this point in his famous experiments involving judgments of the lengths of straight lines drawn on cards, in which he found that most group members were willing, at least once, to defer to the group's clearly false judgments, at least when members of the group were otherwise unanimous.[18] In other words, people were prepared to ignore the evidence of their own senses in order to agree with everyone else. If people will ignore their own visually clear perceptions of simple straight lines and defer to others, then surely they are likely to defer to others on the hard and complicated questions that face businesses and governments.

Here too, the group is at risk of throwing away information that it needs. It has to find a way to get an honest answer to this question: What do you see?

Social Incentives

The second reason for self-silencing involves the consequences of speaking up and dissenting. People might be silent not because they think that they must be wrong (as in the case of informational pressure), but instead to avoid the risk of social punishment of various sorts. In fact, social influences undoubtedly contributed to self-silencing in the Kennedy White House. Even in societies and organizations that are strongly committed to freedom and honesty, people who defy the dominant position within the group risk a form of disapproval that will lead them to be less trusted, less liked, and less respected in the future.

Leaders have a lot of influence here. If your boss thinks that some proposition is true, you will not want to say that it is false. Businesses and governments inevitably have hierarchies, and those who are high in the hierarchy tend to command agreement from those who work for them. The higher-ups send a signal: *Disagree with me at your peril.* They might send an equally damaging signal: *Complicate my life at your peril.* Or their body language might suggest: *I am very busy.* Even if your boss has not yet said what she thinks, it's not likely that you will want to speak out in defiance of the views of most of your colleagues.

Most of us have seen these dynamics in action, and many of us have been subject to them ourselves. If certain group members who serve as leaders are willing and able to impose social punishments, others will be unlikely to defy them publicly. (This, by the way, is one reason that smart leaders often speak last, after they hear from everyone else. As Sunstein can attest, even presidents tend to let others speak first. More on this later.) Similarly, a large majority will impose more social pressure than a small one.

A Framework: The Benefits— and Costs—of Speaking Up

We can put these points into a more general framework. Suppose that group members are deliberating about some question—say, what will happen in two months if the group continues on its current course. Suppose, too, that each member has some information that bears on the answer to that question. Will the members be willing to disclose what they know?

For each group member, the answer is likely to depend on the individual benefits and the individual costs of disclosure. In some cases, of course, people who disclose information to the group will end up benefiting a lot. They can win respect, admiration, and status. They might end up with a promotion. Wise groups, and the leaders of such groups, let people know that when members help to produce better decisions, they will be rewarded. When groups follow this practice, they change the individual's calculus by increasing the private benefits of disclosure.

But many groups are not so wise. In some groups, people who disclose information will end up gaining a lot less than the group itself will. If you have information that is jarring or disruptive, and you speak out, your colleagues might look at you funny or like you a bit less. In this sense, participants in group deliberation face a social dilemma, in which each person, following his or her rational self-interest, will *not* tell the group what it needs to know. At least this is so if each member receives only a small portion of the benefits that come to the group from a good outcome.

This unfortunate situation faces many institutions, including corporate boards, religious organizations, and government agencies. Much of the time, the institution, and not the individual, is the big winner from a good decision. Think, for example, of a young lawyer who is prepared to tell senior members of a law firm that their current litigation strategy is way off course. It may well be that the young lawyer will risk her own position inside the firm, and the potential winner—the firm itself—is unwilling to reward that particular malcontent, at least in the short run.

Altruism and social norms can be helpful here. In government, for example, people may well end up disclosing their doubts and the information that supports those doubts, even if they will not gain a thing from the disclosure. The reason? They are patriots. They want to do their job well.

In government, a number of civil servants Sunstein knew within the Office of Management and Budget had no obvious political affiliation, cared about the public interest, and were willing to tell political leaders (including Sunstein) that they were just wrong. One example is Kevin Neyland, the longtime deputy administrator of OIRA—political affiliation unknown, integrity unmatched, a kind and heroic soul with a willingness to ruffle feathers. Because Neyland often saw worst-case scenarios, Sunstein nicknamed him Eeyore, after the gloomy pessimist in Winnie-the-Pooh. For political leaders, the Kevin Neylands of the world are indispensible, even if they aren't always a lot of fun.

The upshot is that if people are motivated by commitments or character to follow a sometimes self-sacrificing, helpful norm ("Tell the group what you know"), the absence of private benefits may not be a terrible problem. But in many groups, it is hazardous to rely on altruism, and prevailing group norms don't always favor expressing your doubts.

It gets worse if the statements of other group members suggest that the information held by a would-be dissenter is probably wrong or unhelpful. If so, then the private benefit of disclosure is reduced far more. In that event, the potential dissenter has good reason to believe that disclosure would be just a waste and would not improve the group's decision at all. Things are even worse if those who speak against the apparent consensus will suffer some kind of reputational injury (or more). If they will lose the confidence of their colleagues or their boss, they have a lot to gain from shutting up.

In that event, the private calculus is straightforward: silence is golden. With a fuller understanding of that calculus, we can now see why group members will often go along with the apparent consensus. Under reasonable assumptions, they will not benefit from speaking out, and they might even be harmed. And in any case, they might just be wrong.

In the discussion thus far, we have been assuming that group members have facts and opinions and that the question is whether they should stay quiet. That's a useful simplifying assumption, but sometimes group members just aren't sure what they think. The question, then, is whether they should go out and learn, perhaps by doing a little research and inquiring about the views of others, including those outside their group.

If other group members seem pretty sure about what is true, you might think, *What's the point of trying to learn something new? Wouldn't that be a waste?* And if other group members don't want alternative views and might punish those who venture them, it might make sense to ask the same questions. We will emphasize how groups can learn what their members know. Our discussion will also explore how groups can encourage their members to learn and to transmit to the group what they find. In part 2, we investigate some adventurous ways that members might do exactly that.

Self-Censorship

Suppose that your own ultimate conclusion goes in one direction, but that you have information suggesting that your conclusion may not be right. On balance, you have reached a certain conclusion, but you have knowledge cutting in both directions. What will you do? Will you inform members of your group of everything that you know or only what supports your conclusion?

The evidence suggests that in such circumstances, people have a strong tendency to self-censor. When people have information that conflicts with their own conclusion, they tend not to share that information with others. One study of over five hundred mock jury deliberations almost *never* observed a juror contributing information that contradicted his or her currently preferred verdict.[19] This form of self-censorship is an independent problem, because it can deprive groups of crucial information. Groups and their leaders need to know not only about people's conclusions, but also about the assortment of factors that led to those conclusions.

Self-censorship of this kind may occur as part of a deliberate strategy to persuade: it would be counter to your interests to provide information that contradicts your own conclusions. Why on earth would you give ammunition to the other side? But the same result can occur even when the speaker has the best of intentions. Group members do not have a lot of motivation to share information that they themselves have already discounted in reaching their own conclusion. Their reluctance to share stems not from instrumental or strategic factors, but from a sense that it would be counterproductive to share information that they themselves deem false, misleading, or invalid. In a way, that conclusion is pretty reasonable—but here again, groups are being deprived of knowledge, and potentially important knowledge, that their own members have.

Minorities and Low Status

Both informational pressures and social influences help to explain the finding that in a deliberating group, people who are in a minority position often silence themselves or otherwise have disproportionately little weight. There is a more particular finding: members of low-status groups—less educated people, African Americans, and sometimes women—speak less and carry less influence within deliberating groups than do their higher-status peers.[20]

Both informational influences and social pressures, likely to be especially strong for low-status members, contribute to this result. Once more, the unfortunate consequence can be a loss of information to the group as a whole, thus ensuring that deliberating groups do far worse than they would if only they could aggregate the information held by group members.

Let us now turn to the four major sources of group failures.

2

Amplifying Errors

No one would get a Nobel Prize for demonstrating that human beings make mistakes. Yet we have noted that in recent decades, behavioral scientists have done a lot of work to specify how and when people err. And in fact, at least five Nobel Prizes in Economics have been won by scientists associated with behavioral economics; the winners include Daniel McFadden in 2000, George Akerlof in 2001, Daniel Kahneman in 2002, Thomas Schelling in 2005, and Robert Shiller in 2013.

Garbage In? A Brief Guided Tour

The real advances can be found in efforts to specify exactly why and when human beings go wrong—in identifying the mechanisms that lead people to err. We know that people use heuristics, or mental shortcuts, that lead them to make predictable errors. People are also subject to identifiable biases, which produce systematic errors.[1] As we have noted, both heuristics and biases can be connected with the family of cognitive operations known as System 1—the intuitive, automatic system that works fast and without a lot of effort. Our main interest here is in group behavior, and in providing a guided tour, we emphasize the heuristics and biases that are most relevant to what groups do, especially in the domains of business and government.

Availability

Human beings err because they use the *availability heuristic* to answer difficult questions about probability. How likely is a terrorist attack, a hurricane, a traffic jam, an accident from a nuclear power plant, a sexually transmitted disease? How likely is it that a particular product or reform will succeed? That a new film or television show will flop or attract a big audience?

When people use the availability heuristic, they answer a question of probability by asking whether examples come readily to mind. People tend to say that on a random printed page, more words will end with the letters *ing* than with the letter *n* in the second-to-last position. This is an obviously incorrect judgment, made because words ending with *ing* are easy to call to mind.[2] Such findings bear on private and public responses to risks— suggesting, for example, that people will be especially responsive to the dangers of crime, earthquakes, and environmental disasters because examples are easy to recall.

In business and government, people often respond to yesterday's famous failure (or celebrated success). If a particular strategy or approach turned out disastrously, it will be very much in mind, and today's decision will be made in light of that disaster. No politician wants to be responsible for "another Vietnam" or to be "another Neville Chamberlain." Foreign policy is sometimes made by reference to available analogies—not the worst approach in the world, but a pretty unreliable one. If a company put a lot of money into a recent flop, the firm is likely to try to avoid a new initiative that looks even a little bit like the flop, even if the new initiative has a lot of promise. The availability heuristic can lead people in bad directions; it's a lot worse than a careful statistical analysis.

This heuristic also explains some of the sources of discrimination on the basis of race, sex, age, and disability. If it is easy to bring to mind cases in which a female employee quit work to care for her family, sex discrimination is more likely. And whenever a company makes employment-related decisions, there is a risk that the availability heuristic will produce mistakes. Good decisions rely on the full performance record, not on snapshot impressions or on whether a candidate is reminiscent of someone who failed or succeeded. In fact, Michael Lewis's best seller, *Moneyball*, is a terrific case study of this point, showing that statistical analysis is a lot better than personal impressions in the evaluation of base-ball talent—a finding that applies to the evaluation of talent of all kinds.

In this way, *familiarity* can affect the availability of instances. But *salience* is important as well. A terrorist attack shown on television will be vivid and highly salient to viewers and will have a greater impact than a report about the attack in the newspaper.[3] The point helps explain a lot of human behavior. For example, whether people will buy insurance for natural disasters is greatly affected by recent experiences.[4] In the aftermath of an earthquake, people suddenly become far readier to buy insurance for earthquakes—but their readiness to do so declines steadily from that point on, as vivid memories recede.

Use of the availability heuristic is far from irrational, but it can easily lead to serious errors of fact. After a flood or a hurricane, it is predictable that people will take significant steps to prepare for floods or hurricanes—and also possible that before any low-probability disaster, they will take inadequate precautions or maybe none at all. If companies use the availability heuristic, they may well make significant mistakes, at least if they make excessive generalizations from events that are recent or readily called to mind.

Emphasizing the success of the Oakland Athletics general manager Billy Beane, Lewis's *Moneyball* points to the importance, in baseball, of relying not on intuition, emotions, anecdotes, or even experience, but on careful statistical analysis. The "Moneyball" idea is being applied in many domains, including government itself. Decision makers do a lot better playing their own version of Moneyball than they do using the availability heuristic. We might well see Moneyball as a strategy to strengthen the hand of System 2, using it as a safeguard against the mistakes of System 1.

Representativeness

Most people also follow the *representativeness heuristic*, which means that our judgments about probability are influenced by assessments of resemblance or similarity (the extent to which A looks like B, physically or otherwise).[5] You might think that a prospective job candidate "looks like" a good CEO, and this thought might greatly affect your judgment. Some seasoned baseball scouts, for example, tend to focus on whether a prospect looks like a ballplayer. Billy Beane liked to respond, "We're not selling jeans here." Rejecting the representativeness heuristic, he examined players' statistics, not their game films.

The representativeness heuristic is famously exemplified by people's answers to questions about the likely career of a hypothetical woman named Linda, described as follows: "Linda is thirty-one years old, single, outspoken, and very bright. She majored in philosophy. As a student, she was deeply concerned with issues of discrimination and social justice and also participated in antinuclear demonstrations."[6] People were asked to rank, in order of probability, eight possible futures for Linda. Most of these were fillers (such as psychiatric social worker, elementary school teacher); the two crucial ones were "bank teller" and "bank teller and active in the feminist movement."

Most people said that Linda was less likely to be a bank teller than to be a bank teller and active in the feminist movement. This is an obvious mistake, a logical fallacy in the form of a *conjunction error*, in which two characteristics A *and* B are thought to be more likely than characteristic A alone. The error stems from the representativeness heuristic: Linda's description seems to match our stereotypes of "bank teller and active in the feminist movement" far better than "bank teller." The representativeness heuristic helps explain what social scientists Paul Rozin and Carol Nemeroff have called "sympathetic magical thinking," including the beliefs that some objects (especially disgusting ones) have contagious properties and that causes resemble their effects.[7] The representativeness heuristic often works well, but in business and politics, it can also lead to severe blunders. Hiring decisions often go badly wrong because of the use of representativeness.

Relying on representativeness, as in the case of Linda, rather than on a more systematic, rational process can produce stereotyped thinking, again leading to mistakes. Malcolm Gladwell cites the historical example of people's exaggerated estimation of Warren G. Harding's capacity for leadership, simply because he looked so "presidential"; his appearance and demeanor matched our prototype of a political leader.[8] Other "halo effects," such as the tendency to vote for candidates who look competent or who are simply taller, again matching our mental image of a prototypical leader, are partly a product of the representativeness heuristic.[9]

Framing

Human beings are subject to *framing effects*, which means that their decisions are influenced by how a decision is framed, even though the different frames reflect merely semantic differences rather than reality. By a "frame," we mean to refer to how a problem is presented to someone, or how people represent or define a decision from their own perspective. The same decision can be thought of in terms of "What is lost?" or "What is gained?" or in terms of "What should I choose?" or "What should I reject?" The key point is that the frame has a big effect on what is ultimately decided. For example, people are more likely to have an operation if they are told that after five years, 90 percent of people are alive than if they are told that after five years, 10 percent of people are dead. A meat product advertised as "90 percent fat-free" is far more appealing than one advertised as "10 percent fat." If people are told that they will "save $600 per year" if they use energy conservation approaches, they are less likely to use such approaches than if they are told that if they decline to do so, they will "lose $600 per year."

Perhaps the most interesting manifestation of gain-loss framing effects is a subtle impact on our appetite for risk taking ("are alive" induces the gain frame, "are dead" the loss frame; "90 percent fat-free" is gain, "10 percent fat" is loss). Sometimes, sadly, we do face options that are most obviously seen as losses from our current circumstances. If a decision dilemma is framed in terms of losses for both alternatives, most people shift from a cautious, risk-avoiding attitude to become risk seeking. This is especially true if some of the possible but uncertain outcomes associated with a course of action get us back to the status quo or break-even condition. Most obviously, this point explains some of the crazy bets that gamblers play, in a usually futile effort just to get back to where they started, but there are many socially more consequential examples in medical, business, and government decisions.

We can debate whether and to what extent it is rational for people to be so vulnerable to how problems are framed. But there is no doubt that individuals can be nudged by descriptions of choices, even if the more effective descriptions involve clever uses of words, rather than substantive differences.

Egocentric Bias and More

If you are like most people, you suffer from *egocentric bias*—the bias that leads most of us to think that other people think and act as we do. We exaggerate the extent to which our tastes and preferences are typical. When asked what percentage of other people go to the movies on Saturday night, love Bob Dylan or Taylor Swift, favor a particular political candidate, or think that the latest Steven Spielberg movie will win the Oscar, most of us show a bias in the direction that we ourselves favor.

This bias leads to major mistakes. For example, people who support any particular candidate typically overestimate the candidate's chances of success. Even though this has happened before, it will happen again; it's hard to avoid the bias. The same problem can arise in firms, as people think that if they love a product, other people are going to love it too. Since people who make products often love what they make, they might well end up overestimating its appeal to others.

We have referred to other biases as well, and while each has produced an extensive literature, we will rest content with a few additional notes of special importance to business (but also, as it happens, romantic relationships).[10] If the course of an action is failing, people tend to increase their commitment to it, rather than simply cutting their losses. Human beings are prone to *unrealistic optimism*. About 90 percent of drivers have been found to believe that they are safer than the average driver. With respect to most of the risks that human beings face, people typically think that their prospects are a bit better than reality warrants.

So too, human beings are prone to *overconfidence*, not least when they make investment decisions. Thus, they exhibit a habit of overprecision, believing that their forecasts are more accurate and precise than in fact they are. What's your best estimate of the value of a favorite investment at the end of the year? You might say, "$74 per share." Now, what is your 90 percent confidence interval around that estimate, such that you will be surprised only 10 percent of the time by an actual value outside that interval? If you are a typical investor, you will be surprised far more than 10 percent of the time.[11]

We have mentioned the *planning fallacy*, which is closely associated with both optimism and overconfidence.[12] Projects small (term papers) and large (the Big Dig tunnel in Boston, the Sochi Olympics site) invariably run over budget and take much longer to complete than the original plans. When companies try to make valid cost estimates, even for routine projects, they often use multipliers of greater than two, but their estimates are still too low. The error arises from a myopic focus on one scenario for the project, which blocks off thoughts about the myriad of contingencies—interruptions from competing commitments, supply-chain failures, unexpected failures by partners, "acts of god" like weather conditions, and so on—and thus produces a coherent, overoptimistic narrative.

Human beings also suffer from *hindsight bias*, which means that when things turn out a certain way, they tend to think, *I knew it all along.*[13] A real problem with hindsight bias is that it can decrease the likelihood of learning. If I am not surprised by the outcome, because hindsight falsely tells me I already knew what would happen, I will not put any thought into revising my beliefs about the situation. The next time I am confronted with a similar judgment, I repeat my mistake.

Finally, people fall prey to the *sunk-cost fallacy*, which means that they do not act rationally with respect to costs that they have already paid out.[14] If I invest in concert tickets (or health club memberships or a war), I am motivated to stay the course, even when I lose interest or when it is obvious (at least from outside the endeavor) that I am involved in a losing proposition. We will explore some potential remedies for this fallacy, and for others, in part 2.

Garbage Out

For our purposes here, a central and even crucial question is whether groups avoid the errors made by individuals. Often they do not—providing vivid illustrations of the principle "garbage in, garbage out," in a way that mocks the aspiration to collective correction of individual blunders. In fact, individual errors are not merely replicated but actually *amplified* in many group decisions—a process of "some garbage in, much garbage out."

Here is an especially disturbing finding, one with great relevance to group behavior in both business and politics: groups are even more likely than individuals to escalate their commitment to a course of action that is failing—and all the more so if members identify strongly with the groups of which they are a part.[15] We know that when things start to go awry, some individuals ramp up their commitment to their original plan, in part because of a strong emotional commitment to making the plan work.

Groups are even worse on this count. There is a clue here to why companies, states, and even nations often continue with projects and plans that are clearly failing. If a company is marketing a product that is selling poorly, it may continue on its misguided course simply because of group dynamics. So too with a nation whose economic policy or approach to foreign affairs is hurting its citizens.

We noted that with respect to the planning fallacy, groups are also worse than individuals—a finding that reflects the risk that groups will be far too optimistic. Groups have also been found to have the following problems:

- They amplify, rather than weaken, reliance on the representativeness heuristic.[16]

- They show more unrealistic overconfidence than do individual group members.[17]

- They are even more vulnerable to framing effects than are individuals.[18]

- They are more affected by spurious arguments from lawyers.[19]

- They are even more susceptible to the sunk-cost fallacy.[20]

In a revealing finding that bears on the power of the representativeness heuristic, groups have been found to make more, rather than fewer, conjunction errors (the belief that two events together are more likely to occur than either one of the events alone) than do individuals, when individual error rates are high. Conversely, groups make fewer conjunction errors when individual error rates are low.[21]

Similar biases infect the legal system. Suppose, for example, that individual jurors are biased because of pretrial publicity that misleadingly implicates the defendant or even because of the defendant's unappealing physical appearance. If so, juries are likely to amplify rather than correct those individual biases.[22] This point is not restricted to juries; it has implications for group decisions of all kinds. If individuals in a firm are somehow biased by irrelevant or invalid evidence, the group may well be more biased still.

We don't want to leave the impression that every judgment bias is amplified by groups. For some biases, groups repeat the individual error, but do not increase it, and for others, they might even decrease it. Compared with individuals, groups have been found to demonstrate a slightly lower level of reliance on the availability heuristic (recall that this heuristic can lead to clear errors).[23] And people's tendency to anchor on salient numbers ("anchoring bias") is somewhat reduced by group deliberation, as are the hindsight and egocentric biases. The larger point, however, is that individual biases are not systematically corrected at the group level and they often get worse.

Why More Garbage?

Why are individual errors so often amplified and so infrequently corrected at the group level? Return to our two themes: informational pressures and social influences. Both are at work.

Suppose that most members of a group are prone to make specific errors. If the majority makes those errors, then most people will see others making the same errors. What they see will work as "social proof," conveying information about what is right. Those who are not specialists are likely to think, *If most people make the same errors, maybe they are not errors at all.* Social influences also play a role. If most group members make errors, other members also might make them simply not to seem disagreeable or foolish. When groups amplify the blunders of their members, social influence is a large reason.

To be sure, there is some good news, in the form of evidence that deliberating groups can correct or reduce certain biases. We have seen that for "eureka" problems, groups do well, even if individual members begin with an answer produced by some kind of bias. This is an important finding. As we will see, it has implications for how groups can do better. If group members recognize that an answer, once announced, is clearly right, they will tend to converge on it. This convergence on the truth can occur for three reasons. First, people sometimes just recognize the answer as right; it is somewhere in their minds, but they haven't had access to it, so there is a sudden click of recognition. Second, the person who announces the right answer may be able to demonstrate its validity, perhaps with a compelling argument or a logical derivation. And finally, the technical authority of the person is sometimes indisputable. When estimating a fact about traffic, a highway engineer is the authority; about medicine, the physicians are the experts. This raises a nice question: How can groups become more likely to say some version of "eureka"?

Groups will also do better than individuals in overcoming egocentric bias. The reason is straightforward. As an individual, you will focus on your own tastes—on what you like and what you don't like. Maybe you are wildly excited about a new Captain America movie, or maybe you think that a new cell phone, bright pink and shaped in a circle with Ronald Reagan's picture on it, is awesome and impossible to resist. If you consult with others, you are likely to find out that your own taste is idiosyncratic. (One of us agrees with you, though, about a new Captain America movie.)

The broader lesson is that if groups are able to benefit from having diverse views, people will quickly learn that their own position is not universally held, and hence the bias is reduced. In these cases, group deliberation supplies an important corrective. Note that we're less likely to get that corrective if the group consists of like-minded people, where egocentric bias might be amplified.

This is probably why the availability bias is slightly reduced in groups. Maybe the group members all rely on what comes to mind, but the members are likely to have different memories, yielding a more representative sample of salient information at the group level. Or consider the hindsight bias. Compared with individuals, groups are slightly less susceptible to that bias.[24] Group members who are not susceptible to hindsight bias may be able to persuade others that it is indeed a bias, or perhaps some members were surprised by the outcome (which reduces the individual hindsight effect).

But the larger point is that with group discussion, individual errors are often propagated and amplified rather than eliminated. When individuals show a high degree of bias, groups are likely to be more biased, not less biased, than their median or average member. Here, then, is a major reason that groups fail.

CHAPTER

3

Cascades

Researchers have long known that errors in groups can be amplified if their members influence one another. Of course, the human animal is essentially sociable, and human language may be the most subtle and engaging social mechanism in the animal kingdom. The brain is wired to help us naturally synchronize with and imitate other human beings from birth.[1] Emotions are contagious in our species; obesity appears to be contagious too, and the same may well be true for happiness itself.[2] (We know a behavioral economist who offers what he calls a law of human life: "You cannot be happier than your spouse.") It is no exaggeration to say that *herding* is the fundamental behavior of human groups.

If you are doubtful, consider a brilliant study of music downloads.[3] Sociologist Matthew Salganik and his coauthors conclude that there is a lot of serendipity in which music succeeds and which fails, and that small differences in early popularity make a major difference in ultimate success. In business, many people are aware of this point—but not nearly aware enough. They underrate the extent to which success or failure depends on what happens shortly after launch and frequently overrate the contributions of intrinsic merit.

Here's how Salganik's study worked. The researchers created a control group in which people could hear and download one or more of forty-eight songs by new bands. In the control group, intrinsic merit and personal tastes drove the choices. Individuals were not told anything about what anyone else had downloaded or liked. They were left to make their own independent judgments about which songs they liked. To test the effect of social influences, Salganik and his coauthors also created eight other subgroups. In each of these subgroups, each member could see how many people had previously downloaded individual songs in his or her particular subgroup.

In short, Salganik and his colleagues were testing the relationship between social influences and consumer choices. What do you think happened? Would knowledge of others' choices make a difference, in terms of ultimate numbers of downloads, if people could see the behavior of others?

The answer is that it made a huge difference. While the worst songs (as established by the control group) never ended up at the very top and the best songs never ended up at the very bottom, *essentially anything else could happen.* If a song benefited from a burst of early downloads, it could do really well. If it did not get that benefit, almost any song could be a failure. As Salganik and Duncan Watts later demonstrated, you can manipulate outcomes pretty easily, because popularity is a self-fulfilling prophecy.[4] This means that if a site shows (falsely) that a song is being downloaded a lot, that song can get a tremendous boost and eventually become a hit. John F. Kennedy's father, Joe Kennedy, was said to have purchased tens of thousands of early copies of his son's book, *Profiles in Courage*. The book became a best seller. Smart dad.

There's a lesson here both for businesses that seek to market products and for foolish groups whose leaders often announce a preference for a proposed course of action before the groups have gathered adequate information or aired possible outcomes. The lesson seems obvious, but it now has a solid empirical foundation: if a project, business, politician, or cause gets a lot of early support, it can turn out to be the group's final preference, even if it would fail on its intrinsic merits without that support. Both small and large groups can be moved in this way. If the initial speakers in a group favor a particular course of action, the group may well end up favoring that position, even if it would not have done so if the initial speakers had been different.

When products succeed, we often think that their success was inevitable. Wasn't the *Mona Lisa* bound to be one of the most famous and admired paintings in the world? Isn't her portrait uniquely mysterious and irresistible? Weren't the Beatles destined for success? The Harry Potter series is one of the most popular in the history of publishing. The books are great; how could it be otherwise? Beware of this way of thinking, because inevitability is often an illusion. We can't prove it here, but it's true: with a few twists of fate, you would never have heard of the *Mona Lisa*, the Beatles, or even Harry Potter. (In fact, each of these now iconic works had inauspicious beginnings, but were bumped into the limelight by unpredictable bursts of popularity.)

For their part, many groups end up with a feeling of inevitability, thinking that they were bound to converge on what ultimately became their shared view. Beware of that feeling too, because it is often an illusion. The group's conclusion might well be an accident of who spoke first—and hence of what we might call an incidental side effect of the group's discussions. An agenda that says "bosses go first" might produce very different outcomes from one that says "subordinates go first."

Savvy managers are often entirely aware of this point and organize the discussion so that certain people speak at certain times. Within the federal government, some of the most effective leaders are masters of this process. They know that if, at a crucial juncture, they call on the person with whom they agree, they can sway the outcome. Lesson for managers: devote some thought to the speakers with whom you agree, and get them to speak early and often. Another lesson for managers: don't do that if you don't know what the right answer is.

Up-Votes and Down-Votes

Other research supports our central point (and also helps to dispel the illusion of inevitability). Lev Muchnik, a professor at Hebrew University of Jerusalem, and his colleagues carried out an ingenious experiment on a website that displays a diverse array of stories and allows people to post comments, which can in turn be voted up or down. With respect to the posted comments, the website compiles an aggregate score, which comes from subtracting the number of down-votes from the number of up-votes. To put a metric on the effects of social influences, the researchers explored three conditions: (1) "up-treated," in which a comment, when it appeared, was automatically and artificially given an immediate up-vote; (2) "down-treated," in which a comment, when it appeared, was automatically and artificially given an immediate down-vote; and (3) "control," in which comments did not receive any artificial initial signal. Millions of site visitors were randomly assigned to one of the three conditions. The question: What would be the ultimate effect of an initial up-vote or down-vote?

You might well think that after so many visitors (and hundreds of thousands of ratings), a single initial vote could not possibly matter. Some comments are good, and some comments are bad, and in the end, quality will win out. It's a sensible thought, but if you thought it, you would be wrong. After seeing an initial up-vote (and recall that it was entirely artificial), the next viewer became 32 percent more likely also to give an up-vote. What's more, this effect persisted over time. After five months, a single positive initial vote artificially increased the mean rating of comments by a whopping 25 percent! It also significantly increased turnout (the total number of ratings).

With respect to negative votes, the picture was not symmetrical—an intriguing finding. True, the initial down-vote did increase the likelihood that the next viewer would also give a down-vote. But that effect was rapidly corrected. After the same period of five months, the artificial down-vote had zero effect on median ratings (though it did increase turnout). Muchnik and his colleagues conclude that "whereas positive social influence accumulates, creating a tendency toward ratings bubbles, negative social influence is neutralized by crowd correction." They think that their findings have implications for product recommendations, stock-market predictions, and electoral polling. Maybe an initial positive reaction, or just a few such reactions, can have major effects on ultimate outcomes—a conclusion very much in line with Salganik's study of popular music.

We should be careful before drawing large lessons from one or two studies, particularly when no money was on the line. But there is no question that when groups move in the direction of some products, people, political initiatives, and ideas, the movement may not be because of their intrinsic merits, but because of the functional equivalent of early up-votes. There are lessons here about the extraordinary unpredictability of groups—and about their frequent lack of wisdom. Of course, Muchnik's study involved very large groups, but the same thing can happen in small ones. In fact, the effect can be even more dramatic in small groups, as an initial up-vote—in favor of some plan, product, or verdict— has a large effect on other votes.

How Many Murders?

Here's a clean test of group wisdom and social influences. As we saw in chapter 1, the median estimate of a large group is often amazingly accurate (and we will return to that theme in chapter 8). But what happens if people in the group know what others are saying? You might think that knowledge of this kind will help, but the picture is a lot more complicated.

Jan Lorenz, a researcher in Zurich, worked with several colleagues to learn what happens when people are asked to estimate certain values, such as the number of assaults, rapes, and murders in Switzerland.[5] The researchers found that when people are informed about the estimates of others, there is a significant reduction in the diversity of opinions—a result that tends to make the crowd *less* wise. (Note, however, that even with diminished diversity, the crowd is still somewhat more accurate than a typical individual.[6]) Lorenz and his coauthors found another problem with the crowd, which is that because people hear about other estimates, they also become more confident. Notably, people received monetary payments for getting the right answer, so their mistakes were consequential—not just an effort to curry favor with others. The authors conclude that for decision makers, the advice given by a group "may be thoroughly misleading," at least when group members are interacting with one another.

Notwithstanding their differences, the Salganik, Muchnik, and Lorenz studies have one thing in common: they all involve social cascades. A cascade occurs when people influence one another, so much so that participants ignore their private knowledge and rely instead on the publicly stated judgments of others. Corresponding to our two accounts of social influences, there are two kinds of cascades: informational and reputational. In informational cascades, people silence themselves out of respect for the information conveyed by others. In reputational cascades, people silence themselves to avoid the opprobrium of others.

Informational Cascades

Cascades need not involve deliberation, but deliberative processes and group decisions often involve cascades. The central point is that those involved in a cascade do not reveal all that they know. As a result, the group does not obtain important information, and it often decides badly.[7]

Informational Cascades in Action

To see how informational cascades work, imagine a company whose officials are deciding whether to authorize some new venture.[8] Let us assume that the group members are announcing their views in sequence, a common practice in face-to-face teams and committees everywhere. Every member has some private information about what should be done. But each also attends, reasonably enough, to the judgments of others.

Andrews is the first to speak. He suggests that the venture should be authorized. Barnes now knows Andrews's judgment. It is clear that she, too, should vote in favor of the venture if she agrees independently with Andrews. But suppose that her independent judgment is otherwise. Everything depends on how much confidence she has in Andrews's judgment and how much confidence she has in her own. Suppose that she trusts Andrews no more and no less than she trusts herself. If so, she should be indifferent about what to do and might simply flip a coin. Or suppose that on the basis of her own independent information, she is unsure what to think. If so, she will follow Andrews.

Now turn to a third member, Carlton. Suppose that both Andrews and Barnes have argued in favor of the venture, but that Carlton's own information, though inconclusive, suggests that the venture is probably a bad idea. Here again, Carlton will have to weigh the views of both Andrews and Barnes against his own. On reasonable assumptions, there is a good chance that Carlton will ignore what he knows and follow Andrews and Barnes. After all, it seems likely, in these circumstances, that both Andrews and Barnes had reasons for their conclusion. Unless Carlton thinks that his own information is better than theirs, he should follow their lead. If he does, Carlton is in a cascade.

If Carlton is quite savvy, he might consider the possibility that Barnes deferred to Andrews's judgment and did not make any kind of independent judgment. If so, Carlton might ignore the fact that Barnes agreed with Andrews. But in the real world, many group members do not consider the possibility that earlier speakers deferred to the views of still earlier ones. People tend to think that if two or more other people believe something, each has arrived at that belief independently.[9] This is an error, but a lot of us make it.

Now suppose that Carlton goes along with Andrews and Barnes, and that group members Davis, Edwards, and Francis know what Andrews, Barnes, and Carlton said and did. On reasonable assumptions, they will do exactly what Carlton did: favor the venture regardless of their private information (which, we are supposing, is relevant but inconclusive). This will happen even if Andrews initially blundered. Again, Davis, Edwards, or Francis might be able to step back and wonder whether Andrews, Barnes, and Carlton really have made independent judgments. But if they are like most people, they will not do that. The sheer weight of the apparently shared view of their predecessors will lead them to go along with the emerging view.

If this is what is happening, we have a now-familiar problem: those who are in the cascade do not disclose the information that they privately hold. In the example just given, decisions will not reflect the overall knowledge or the aggregate knowledge of people in the group—even if the information held by individual members, if actually revealed and aggregated, would produce a quite different (and possibly much better) result. The venture will be authorized even if it is a terrible idea and even if group members know that it is a terrible idea. The simple reason is that people are following the lead of those who came before. Subsequent speakers might fail to rely on, and fail to reveal, private information that actually exceeds the information collectively held by those who started the cascade.

Here's an example of an informational cascade in jury deliberation. One of us (Hastie) has conducted dozens of mock-jury studies, with thousands of volunteer jurors, many with citizens from big-city jury pools. In these studies, the volunteers allowed themselves to be videotaped while deliberating to verdicts on difficult but typical cases. In many juries (mock and real) the deliberation begins with a straw vote, taken just to see where everyone stands.

In dozens of juries, we observed a scenario like the following. The straw vote would circle the jury table and often would start with a small cascade of two or three jurors favoring, with increasing confidence, the same verdict. Because the researchers collected predeliberation private ballots, we knew which verdict was privately preferred by each of the jurors at the table. Let's suppose that Jurors 1, 2, and 3 endorsed second-degree murder, privately and publicly in the straw vote. But we knew that Juror 4 had voted for not guilty and had indicated the highest level of confidence on the predeliberation ballot.

So, what did Juror 4 do, when confronted with the solid line of three murder verdicts? He paused for a second and then said, "Second degree." At this point, Juror 7, an undecided vote, suddenly spoke up and asked, "Why second degree?" A momentary deer-in-the-headlights expression flitted across Juror 4's face, and then he replied, "Oh, it's just obviously second degree." This scenario stands out as an iconic example of an informational cascade, and we have no doubt that this scenario is played out every day in jury rooms, board rooms, and political conference rooms all over the world.

Anxiety and Cascading

People who are humble, pliable, or complacent are especially likely to fall into a cascade. But anxious people might well shatter it, certainly if it reflects a high degree of optimism. Nancy-Ann DeParle is a gold-medal shatterer of cascades, simply because she asks tough, skeptical questions that force people to rethink. Every group needs some people like that, who wonder: *If lots of people share an opinion on a hard question, might it be because they are following the lead of one or two blunderers? Why are there no dissenters?* (Recall the fiasco at the Bay of Pigs.)

It is important to understand that in relying on the statements or actions of their predecessors, group members are not acting irresponsibly. In fact, informational cascades can occur when members are following rigorously rational thought processes. Group members might well be reacting sensibly to the informational signals they receive. If most people think that the venture is a good idea, it's probably a good idea. You should feel, sensibly, that you need a pretty strong counterargument if you are going to disagree with what your colleagues have said.

But we should not underestimate our tendencies to rely on confidence, our own and others', as a cue for what information deserves the most attention (independent of the validity of that information). One of the most insidious side effects of group decision making is that people believe in wrong *group* decisions more than they believe in incorrect *individual* decisions. The social proof resulting from cascades and (conformity more generally) amplifies everyone's trust in the incorrect outcome.[10] And inputs into the decision process from highly confident or dominant personalities have more impact and increase the esteem accorded to those individuals, regardless of the quality of their contributions.[11]

Urns: Red or Black?

Cascades often occur in deliberating groups in the real world.[12] They are also easy to create in the laboratory. The simplest experiment is artificial but also highly revealing, because it is a stylized version of reality—of what happens every day of every year. The experiment is a bit technical and its details are not exactly captivating, but please do bear with us for a bit, because the details explain a lot about how groups end up going wrong.

The experimenters asked participants to guess whether the experiment was using urn A, which contained two red balls and one white, or instead urn B, which contained two white balls and one red.[13] Participants could earn $2 for a correct decision and hence had an economic incentive to make the right choice.

In each round, one urn was selected. Then a participant was asked to make one (and only one) *private draw* of a ball from the selected urn in each round. The participant recorded on an answer sheet (1) the color of that ball and (2) his or her own decision about which urn was involved. The participant did *not* announce to the group which ball had been drawn, but the person did announce his or her own decision (about the likely urn) to everyone.

Then the ball was returned to the urn and the urn was passed to the next participant for another private draw, which again was not disclosed to anyone else, and for this participant's own decision about the urn, which again was disclosed. This process continued until all the participants had made draws and decisions. At that time, the experimenter announced which urn had actually been used. If the participants had picked the urn only on the basis of their private information, they would have been right 66.7 percent of the time. The point of the experiment was to see whether people would decide to ignore their own draw in the face of the announcements of their predecessors—and to explore whether such decisions led to cascades and errors.

The upshot? In the experiment, cascades often did develop— and they usually produced errors. After a number of individual judgments were revealed, people announced decisions that were not indicated by their private draws but that fit with the majority of previous announcements.[14] More than 77 percent of rounds resulted in cascades, and 15 percent of private announcements did not reveal a "private signal," that is, the information provided by the individual's own private draw. Notably, most people's decisions were rationally based on the available information—but erroneous cascades nonetheless developed.[15]

Table 3-1 shows an example of a cascade that produced an inaccurate outcome (the urn used was actually B, but the first two draws produced a cascade in favor of A).[16]

What is noteworthy here, of course, is that the *total* amount of private information—four whites and two reds—pointed to the correct judgment: urn B. But the existence of the two early signals, producing rational but incorrect judgments, led everyone else to fall in line. Initial misrepresentative signals began a chain of incorrect decisions, and the chain was not broken by more representative signals received later.[17] There is evidence that people eventually tend to break very long cascade chains, but there is no doubt that even short chains can create big trouble, and some long ones do persist.[18]

TABLE 3-1

An informational cascade

	Draw from the urn					
	1	2	3	4	5	6
Private signal	A	A	B	B	B	B
Decision	A	A	A	A	A	A

Source: Marc Willinger and Anthony Ziegelmeyer, "Are More Informed Agents Able to Shatter Informa-tion Cascades in the Lab?" in *The Economics of Networks: Interaction and Behaviours*, ed. Patrick Cohendet et al. (New York: Springer, 1998), 291.

This urn experiment maps directly onto real-world decisions by teams and deliberating groups, in which people rely on the expressed views of their predecessors and hence fail to disclose what they know, to the detriment of the group as a whole. Recall here Salganik's music download experiment, which produced similar results. In that experiment, some songs became popular and others tanked; because there is no accounting for taste, we can't be clear that there were mistakes. But if a group ends up making the wrong decision because of the views of those who spoke first, social influence and herding are undermining the truth.

Reputational Cascades

A reputational cascade has an altogether different dynamic. With this kind of cascade, group members think they know what is right or what is likely to be right, but they nonetheless go along with the group to maintain the good opinions of others. The problem is not that group members are influenced by the information contained in the statements of their predecessors, but that they do not want to face the disapproval of their bosses or their colleagues.

Political correctness, an aspersion often used by the political right in the 1990s (and thereafter), can be found in many places; it is hardly limited to left-leaning institutions of higher education. In both business and government, there is often a clear sense that a certain point of view is the right one to have, and that those who question or reject it, even for purposes of discussion, do so at their peril. They seem difficult or not part of the team. They are viewed as wasting the rest of the group's time. They can be disruptive. In extreme cases, they are seen as misfits. Misfits make the group uncomfortable, but wise groups take steps to protect them

Here's how reputational cascades can arise. Suppose Albert suggests that a company's new project is likely to succeed, and suppose that Barbara concurs with Albert, not because she actually thinks that Albert is right (in fact, she thinks he is wrong), but because she does not wish to seem ignorant, adversarial, or skeptical about that project. If Albert and Barbara seem to agree that the project will go well, Cynthia is not only unlikely to contradict them publicly; she might even appear to share their judgment. Cynthia's reaction arises not because she believes the judgment to be correct (she doesn't), but because she does not want to provoke Albert and Barbara's hostility or lose their good opinion.

It should be easy to see how this process might generate a cascade. Once Albert, Barbara, and Cynthia offer a united front on the issue, their colleague David will be most reluctant to contradict them, even if he thinks they are wrong and has excellent reasons for that belief. In the actual world of group decisions, people may, of course, be uncertain whether publicly expressed statements are a product of independent information, participation in an informational cascade, or reputational pressure. As we have noted, listeners and observers undoubtedly overstate the extent to which the actions of others are based on independent information.

The possibility of reputational cascades is demonstrated by an ingenious variation on the urn experiment outlined above.[19] In this experiment, people had to guess from which urn they had drawn a ball, just as in the earlier experiment (i.e., urn A had two red balls and one white; urn B had two white and one red). The participants were paid $0.25 for a correct decision but $0.75 for a decision that matched the decision of the majority of the group. There were punishments for incorrect and nonconforming answers as well. If people made an incorrect decision, they lost $0.25; if their decision failed to match the group's decision, they lost $0.75.

In this experiment, cascades appeared almost all of the time! No fewer than 96.7 percent of rounds resulted in cascades, and 35.3 percent of people's announcements did not match their private signal. That is, they voted publicly against the signal given by their own draw. And when the draw of a subsequent person contradicted the announcement of the predecessor, 72.2 percent of people matched the first announcement. Table 3-2 shows this version of the experiment (the actual urn was B).[20]

This experiment shows that especially unfortunate results should be expected if people are rewarded not only or not mostly for being correct, but also or mostly for saying or doing what other people say and do. Unfortunately, some groups (often led or constituted by very smart people) do offer such rewards. There are plenty of such groups (even in high-stakes business and government settings). Again, the problem is that people are silencing

TABLE 3-2

Conformity and cascades

	Draw from the urn									
	1	2	3	4	5	6	7	8	9	10
Private signal	A	B	B	B	A	B	B	B	A	B
Decision	A	A	A	A	A	A	A	A	A	A

Source: Angela A. Hung and Charles R. Plott, "Information Cascades: Replication and an Extension to Majority Rule and Conformity-Rewarding Institutions," *American Economic Review* 91 (2001): 1508, 1515.

themselves to fit in and are not revealing the important information they actually have.

Availability Cascades

Thus far, we have assumed that group members are, in a sense, entirely rational. They are listening to one another and paying attention to the informational signals given by their predecessors. True, they care about their reputations and they want to be liked and respected, but there is nothing irrational about that.

As we have noted, however, people use judgment heuristics, which can lead them astray, and people are also subject to biases. For purposes of understanding how cascade effects can go wrong, the most important heuristic involves availability. When a particular event is salient, it can lead to *availability cascades*, by which related ideas spread rapidly from one person to another, eventually producing a widespread belief within a group, whether large or small.[21]

A by-product of availability is *associative blocking* or *collaborative fixation*, whereby strong, highly associated ideas block the recall of other informative ideas. This phenomenon is a big problem when a group sets itself the task of generating creative solutions. The creative, novel thought processes of individual members are suppressed by the strong, available ideas generated by other members. Effective brainstorming requires tactics to avoid this troublesome side effect of availability (see further discussion in part 2).

In the area of risk, availability cascades are common. A particular event—involving a dangerous pesticide, an abandoned hazardous waste dump, a nuclear power accident, an act of terrorism—may become well known to the group, even iconic. If so, the event will alter the group's perceptions of a process, a product, or an activity. In business, availability cascades are familiar. Reports of an event, a dramatic success, or a failure may spread like wildfire within or across firms, leading to a judgment about other apparently similar events or products. If a movie (*Star Wars?*), a television show (*Breaking Bad?*), or a book (*Harry Potter?*) does well, businesses will react strongly, eagerly looking for a proposal or a project that seems similar. And indeed, cascades are highly visible in the television industry in sudden bursts of shows about teenaged vampires or privileged housewives, as managers make decisions that reflect recent successes.[22]

Government officials are subject to availability cascades as well. A bad event (say, Neville Chamberlain's capitulation to Hitler, the Vietnam War, or the financial crisis of 2008) may have long-term effects, simply because it is highly salient. Reminded of it when a current crisis arises, people act to avoid a repeat of the historical outcome.

Of course, the underlying judgments might be correct. Sometimes the past really is prologue. But recall that the availability heuristic is highly unreliable. People might know of an instance in which a risk came to fruition, but the instance may not be representative. Pesticides might be safe in general even if a particular pesticide is not. A well-publicized event involving an abandoned hazardous waste dump may suggest that abandoned hazardous waste dumps are far more dangerous than they actually are.

Availability cascades make businesses and government unrealistically optimistic about some possibilities and unrealistically pessimistic about others. And when availability cascades are involved, groups can move in terrible directions. We're not speaking of groupthink here; the problem is that a well-known cognitive bias is interacting, in destructive ways, with social influences.

4

Group Polarization

There are clear links between cascade effects and the well-established phenomenon of group polarization, by which members of a deliberating group end up adopting a more extreme version of the position toward which they tended before deliberation began.[1] The problem is especially severe for groups of like-minded people, who typically get more extreme as a result of deliberation.

Group polarization is a frequent pattern with deliberating groups. It has been found in hundreds of studies involving more than a dozen countries, including the United States, France, Afghanistan, and Germany.[2] For example, group members who start out by disapproving of the United States, and are suspicious of its intentions, will end up with greater disapproval and suspicion after they exchange points of view. Indeed, there is specific evidence of the latter phenomenon among citizens of France.[3] We are confident that the same phenomenon would be observed if we ran the study in the United States and asked Americans to evaluate the French.

Risky Shifts, Cautious Shifts

The original experiments on the effects of deliberation are especially relevant to businesses and governments alike. The studies involved risk-taking behavior, with a clear finding that people initially inclined to take risks become still more risk-inclined after they deliberate with one another.[4] If group members begin with some willingness to engage in risky behavior, groups will engage in more of that behavior as a result of group discussion. Risky decisions include taking a new job, investing in a foreign country, escaping from a prisoner-of-war camp, or running for political office. With respect to many such decisions, members of deliberating groups became significantly more risk-seeking after a brief period of exchanging views. On the basis of this evidence, the prevailing wisdom was that deliberation produced a systematic *risky shift*.

But later studies drew this conclusion into question—and also created a big puzzle. On many of the same questions on which Americans displayed a risky shift, Taiwanese participants showed a *cautious shift*. Deliberation led citizens of Taiwan to become a lot *less* risk-inclined than they were before they started to talk. And it turned out that among American participants, deliberation sometimes produced a cautious shift, as risk-averse people became more averse to certain risks after they talked with one another, depending on the action they were contemplating. The principal examples of cautious shifts were decisions about whether to marry and whether to board a plane despite severe abdominal pain that would possibly require medical attention. In these cases, the members of deliberating groups, even in the United States, shifted not toward risk but toward greater caution.[5] So much for the idea of a consistent one-directional risky shift!

What explains these unruly findings? A straightforward interpretation reconciles them: the predeliberation median is the best predictor of the direction of the group's shift.[6] When group members are initially disposed toward risk taking, a risky shift is likely. Where members are initially disposed toward caution, a cautious shift is likely. Thus, for example, the striking difference between American and Taiwanese subjects is a product not of cultural habits or a different effect from group deliberation, but of a simple difference in where group members started—more precisely, in the predeliberation medians of the different groups on the key questions. Whereas the Americans started out risk-inclined, the Taiwanese started out risk-averse, and that simple fact explained the different directions of the two shifts. The risky shift and the cautious shift are both subsumed under a single rubric: *group polarization.*

In a finding of special importance for business, group polarization occurs both for matters of fact and for issues of value. Suppose that the question is whether a product will sell a certain number of units in Europe in the next year. If so, group polarization will not be easy to test, simply because the answer is either yes or no, and it is not simple to demonstrate a shift to greater extremism in yes-or-no answers. But suppose that people are asked, on a bounded scale of zero to eight, how likely it is that a product will sell a certain number of units in Europe in the next year, with zero indicating "zero probability," eight indicating "absolutely certain," seven indicating "overwhelmingly likely," six "more probable than not," and five "fifty-fifty."

In that event, the answers from a deliberating group will tend to reveal group polarization, as people move toward more-extreme points on the scale depending on their group's initial median point. If the predeliberation median is six, the group judgment will usually be seven; if the predeliberation median is three, the group judgment will usually be two.[7]

Note here that even federal judges—experts in the law and supposedly neutral—are highly susceptible to group polarization, as both Democratic and Republican appointees show far more ideological voting patterns when sitting with other judges appointed by a president of the same political party.[8] On a three-judge panel, consisting solely of Democratic appointees, Democratic appointees show very liberal voting patterns in cases involving discrimination on the basis of sex and sexual orientation, environmental protection, and the rights of workers—far more liberal patterns than they show when at least one Republican appointee is on a three-judge panel. The pattern is identical for Republican appointees, who show highly conservative voting patterns on all-Republican panels. You can think of three-judge panels as teams, and judicial voting is affected by the attitudinal composition of the team.

Here's a vivid way to see the point. If you want to know how an appellate judge will vote in an ideologically contested case, you might want to find out whether she was appointed by a Republican or a Democratic president. It's a pretty good predictor. But in many areas of the law, here's an even better predictor of how a given judge will vote: Who appointed the other two judges on the panel?

Juries display group polarization as well. In particular, their punitive-damage awards tend to be far higher than the preferred award of the median member, before deliberation. The result of jury deliberation is to produce an increase in extremism, in the particular form of higher awards.[9] There is a lesson here about punishment judgments in general. If group members begin with an inclination to be punitive, there is a good chance that the group will end up more punitive still.

An Experiment in Colorado

To cast light on these questions, the two of us created (along with our friend and colleague David Schkade) a distinctive experiment in group deliberation—one that, we believe, accurately reflects much deliberation in the real world. In this experiment, we recruited citizens from two cities and assembled them into small groups (usually six people), all from the same city. The groups were asked to deliberate on three of the most contested issues of the time: climate change, affirmative action, and same-sex civil unions. The two cities were Boulder, known by its voting patterns to be predominantly liberal (aka "The People's Republic of Boulder"), and Colorado Springs, known by its voting patterns to be predominantly conservative (and nicknamed "The Citadel"). We did a reality check on the participants before the experiment started, ensuring that the Boulder residents were in fact left of center and that the Colorado residents were in fact right of center. The citizens were first asked to record their views individually and anonymously—and then to deliberate together in an effort to reach a group decision. After deliberation, the individual participants were asked to record their postdeliberation views individually and anonymously.

There were three effects from group deliberation:

1. People from Boulder became a lot more liberal on all three issues. By contrast, people from Colorado Springs became a lot more conservative. The effect of group deliberation was to shift individual opinions toward extremism. This shift happened in two ways. First, group "verdicts" on climate change, affirmative action, and same-sex civil unions were more extreme than the predeliberation average of the group members. Second, the *anonymous* views of individual members became more extreme, after deliberation, than were their anonymous views before the participants started to talk. There's a big lesson here. Group deliberation often makes not only groups but also individuals more extreme, so much so that they will state more-extreme views privately and anonymously.

2. Deliberation increased consensus within groups. Before people started to deliberate, many of the groups showed a lot of internal diversity, in the sense that there was considerable divergence in people's individual opinions. Sure, people in Boulder are generally liberal, but in our groups, they did not always agree with one another on the particular issues that we selected. Discussion brought liberals into line with each other, and the same thing happened with conservatives. As a result of a brief period of discussion, group members showed a lot more agreement and less variation in their anonymous postdeliberation expressions of their private views.

3. Deliberation sharply increased the disparities between the views of the largely liberal citizens of Boulder and the largely conservative citizens of Colorado Springs. Before deliberation, there was considerable overlap between many individuals in the two cities. After deliberation, the overlap was a lot smaller. Liberals and conservatives became more sharply divided.

The implications are clear. As a general rule, deliberating groups tend to end up adopting a more extreme position in line with their inclinations before they started to talk, and a major effect of deliberation is to squelch internal diversity—and thus to push different groups apart.

Why Polarization?

Why does group polarization occur? There are three principal reasons.[10]

The first and most important explanation involves the now-familiar idea of informational influence, but with a few twists. Group members pay attention to the arguments made by other group members. The arguments in any group with some initial predisposition will inevitably be skewed in the direction of that predisposition. Suppose, for example, that most group members begin by thinking that a new venture is likely to succeed. If so, there will be a lot of arguments to that effect. As a statistical matter, the arguments favoring the initial position will be more numerous than those pointing in the other direction. Individuals will have thought of or heard of some, but not all, of the arguments that emerge from group deliberation. As a result of the arguments that are made by group members, deliberation will naturally lead people toward a more extreme point in line with what group members initially believed.

The second explanation, also familiar, involves social influences. As we have seen, people want to be perceived favorably by other group members. People's publicly stated views are sometimes a function of how they want to present themselves. Once they hear what others believe, some group members will adjust their positions at least slightly in the direction of the dominant position to preserve their preferred self-presentation. They shift accordingly.[11] If a group's leader or if most group members favor a particular course of action, those who challenge that view do so at their own risk. Here is yet another reason that wise leaders often speak tentatively or not at all, inviting group members to speak their mind.

The third explanation of group polarization is more subtle. It stresses the close links among three factors: confidence, extremism, and corroboration by others.[12] When people lack confidence, they tend to be tentative and therefore moderate, knowing that their own views may be wrong. The great American judge Learned Hand once said that "the spirit of liberty is that spirit which is not too sure that it is right." Tentative people respect the spirit of liberty. But as people gain confidence, they usually become more extreme in their beliefs. The reason is that a significant moderating factor—their own uncertainty about whether they are right—has been eliminated. With respect to group polarization, the key point is that agreement from others tends to increase confidence and, through that route, to increase extremism.

It is partly for this reason, then, like-minded people, having deliberated with one another, become surer that they are right and thus more extreme. In many contexts, people's opinions turn extreme simply because their views have been corroborated and because they become more confident after learning that others share their views.[13] Groups can badly blunder in this way. They might conclude that a new hire is terrific, that a proposed investment is bound to fail, or that a new policy is going to work really well. They end up disappointed, regretful, and often surprised, above all because group dynamics increased their confidence and their conviction.

In Groups, Out Groups, and Shared Identity

A great deal of work suggests that group polarization is more likely and is heightened when people have a sense of shared identity and belong to a tight-knit group or club. This point casts further light on the reasons for group polarization.[14]

In short, people may become polarized because they are attempting to conform to the position that they see as typical within their own group. If their group's identity is made especially salient, the in-group norms are likely to become more extreme.[15] (So if a leader says, "We are all [name a religion]," or "We all built this company together," expect polarization.) And if arguments come from a member of an in-group, they are especially likely to be persuasive. Such arguments just feel right.

People will also be especially fearful of the social pressures that come from rejecting what an in-group member has to say. In a family, a religious organization, a small business, or a company with a sense of identity and hence special insiders, group polarization is particularly likely unless people take special steps to combat it. There is a lesson here for social networks, including those online, where shared identities can be breeding grounds for both confidence and extremism. As a corrective, Alex Pentland of MIT's Media Lab points to the importance not only of engagement, which produces high levels of communication, but also of an appetite for exploration, which promotes seeking out and sharing new information, new opinions, and new solutions.[16]

It should not be a big surprise that the views of out-group members often have little force and might be irrelevant or even suggest that the opposite is true.[17] Should you really listen to someone who belongs to a group that you believe to be silly, bad, or systematically wrong? If your adversaries or competitors say something, you might be more inclined to believe that just the opposite is true.

Consider a test of whether apparently credible media corrections alter the belief, supported and pressed by former Alaska governor Sarah Palin, that the Affordable Care Act would create "death panels."[18] Among those who viewed Palin favorably but had limited political knowledge, the correction turned out to succeed in changing beliefs. The correction also succeeded among those who viewed Palin unfavorably. But the correction actually backfired among Palin supporters with a high degree of political knowledge. After receiving the correction, they became *more* likely to believe that the Affordable Care Act contained death panels. Ironically, the correction intensified their original belief. The study suggests that if members of an out-group support some proposition, their very support might entrench the preexisting beliefs of the in-group.

When out-group members speak out, the reputational pressure is not likely to be strong: Do you really have to worry about the social consequences of rejecting the views of someone usually thought to be wrongheaded, or badly motivated, by people like you? If a self-identified conservative hears arguments from someone who is known to be left of center, those arguments are likely to fall on deaf ears. The clear lesson is that when a group is highly cohesive, and when its members are closely identified with it, polarization is especially likely—and likely to be especially large.

We have clear evidence of this phenomenon among groups of investors; tightly knit investment clubs, unified by social ties, lose a lot of money.[19] Investment clubs do a lot better when their members do not socialize and instead see each other as colleagues rather than friends.

Accuracy

Does group polarization lead to accurate or inaccurate answers? Do deliberating groups err when they polarize?

No simple answer would make sense. Everything depends on the relationship between the correct answer and the group's pre-deliberation tendencies. If the group is leaning toward the right answer, polarization will lead its members directly to the truth. It follows that group polarization might not produce errors or failures at all.

But there are no guarantees here. As a result of group influences, some people will fail to disclose what they know. When individuals are leaning in a direction that is mistaken, the mistake will be amplified by group deliberation. We have encountered troubling examples. When individuals are inclined to commit the planning fallacy, groups are even more likely to commit that fallacy. And when most people are prone to make logical errors, group processes lead to more errors rather than fewer. No one profits from the planning fallacy or logical errors, and group polarization helps to produce a lot of fallacies and plenty of errors.

5

"What Everybody Knows"

Our last group failure may be the most interesting of all. Suppose that group members have a great deal of information—enough to produce the unambiguously right outcome if that information is elicited and properly aggregated. Even if this is so, an obvious problem is that groups will not perform well if they emphasize broadly shared information while neglecting information that is held by one or a few members. Unfortunately, countless studies demonstrate that this regrettable result is highly likely.[1]

Hidden profiles is the technical term for accurate understandings that groups could, but do not, obtain. Hidden profiles are, in turn, a product of the *common-knowledge effect*, through which information held by all group members has more influence on group judgments than information held by only a few members.[2] The most obvious explanation of the effect is the simple fact that as a statistical matter, common knowledge is more likely to be communicated to the group and, as a result, processed and understood by the individual members. But social influences play a big role as well.

Hidden Profiles

Consider a study of serious errors within working groups.[3] The purpose of the study was to see how groups collaborate to make personnel decisions.

Résumés for three candidates applying for a position of marketing manager were placed before group members. The experimenters rigged the attributes of the candidates so that one applicant was clearly the best for the job described. Group members would learn who was best if they were able to see, and to consider, all available information. (The experimenters verified this by forming some control groups in which all subjects were given full information. These groups invariably chose the best candidate.) The subjects were given information packets, each containing a subset of information from the résumés, so that each group member had only part of the relevant information. The groups consisted of three people, some operating face-to-face, some operating online.

Almost none of the deliberating groups made what was conspicuously the right choice! The reason is simple: people failed to share their information in a way that would permit the group to make that choice. Members tended to share positive information about the winning candidate and negative information about the losers. They suppressed negative information about the winner and positive information about the losers. Hence, their statements served to "reinforce the march toward group consensus rather than add complications and fuel debate."[4]

Or consider a simulation of political elections, in which information was parceled out to individual members about three candidates for political office. In this simulation, properly pooled information could have led to what was clearly the best choice, candidate A.[5] In the first condition, each member of the four-person groups was given most of the relevant information (66 percent of the information about each candidate). In that condition, 67 percent of group members favored candidate A before discussion, and 85 percent did so after discussion.[6] This is a clear example of sensible aggregation of information. Groups significantly outperformed individuals, apparently because of the exchange of information and reasons. Here, then, is a clear illustration of the possibility that groups *can* aggregate what members know in a way that produces sensible outcomes.

In the second condition, by contrast, the information that favored candidate A was parceled out to various members of the group so that only 33 percent of the information about each candidate was shared. Furthermore, as the condition was designed, the shared information favored two unambiguously inferior candidates, B and C. In that condition, fewer than 25 percent of group members favored candidate A before discussion—a natural and rational product of the initial distribution of information. But if the unshared information were to emerge through group discussion and were to be taken seriously, the group would end up selecting candidate A. The bad news is that the number of people favoring candidate A actually *fell* after discussion, simply because the shared information had disproportionate influence on group members.[7]

In other words, groups did worse, not better, than individuals when the information was distributed so that the key material was unshared and could emerge only from discussion. Under those circumstances, the shared information was far more influential than the unshared information, to the detriment of the group's ultimate decision.

From this and many similar studies, the general conclusion is that shared information has a far larger impact than unshared information. If everyone in a six-person group has the same information, and if two members have information of their own that everyone else lacks, there is a good chance that the unshared information will never be discussed and shared information will dominate. More specifically, when most of the unshared information is opposed to the position that is initially the most popular, that unshared information will be omitted from the discussion—and will have little influence on what groups end up choosing.[8] Garold Stasser and William Titus, who conducted many relevant experiments, conclude that "group decisions and postgroup preferences reflect the initial preferences of group members *even when the exchange of unshared information should have resulted in substantial shifts in opinion.*"[9]

Nor does discussion increase the recall of unshared information. On the contrary, its major effect is to increase people's recall of the attributes of the initially most popular candidate or position.[10] The most disturbing conclusion is that when key information is unshared, groups are more likely to choose an inferior option after discussion than their individual members might before any discussion occurs.[11]

The Common-Knowledge Effect

These results are best understood as a consequence of the common-knowledge effect, by which information held by all group members has a lot more influence on group judgments than information held by one member or a few.[12] More technically, Stasser and Titus find that the "influence of a particular item of information is directly and positively related to the number of group members who have knowledge of that item before the group discussion and judgment."[13] When information is unshared, group judgments have been found to be no more accurate than the average of the individual judgments, even though—and this is the central point—the groups have possession of more information than do any of the individuals.[14]

The more that information is shared, the more impact it will have as discussion proceeds, precisely because it is more likely to be discussed. In a representative study, deliberating groups failed to elicit and use unshared information, and they would have lost *nothing* in terms of accuracy if they had simply averaged the original judgments of the people involved—a clear finding that deliberation may not improve on the judgments that come from taking statistical averages.[15] (As we have seen, deliberation may also produce worse judgments.)

Cognitively Central, Cognitively Peripheral

Many of the hidden-profile experiments involve volunteer participants from college courses. It is natural to ask: Would the same results be found in the real world?

They would indeed. Consider a study of hiring by high-level executives.[16] In that study, no experimenter controlled the information that the executives had about the various candidates. Instead, the executives' knowledge arose naturally from their own information searches. As a result of those searches, some information was known to all, some was shared by some but not by all, and some was held by only one person.

The result? Even among high-level executives, common information had a disproportionately large impact on discussions and conclusions. The executives gave disproportionately little weight to valuable information held by one person or a few. As a result, the executives made bad decisions, because they did not use the information that their colleagues had.

The same study offers another finding of considerable importance. Some group members are *cognitively central*, in the sense that their personal knowledge is also held by many other group members.[17] What the cognitively central members know, other people know as well. A cognitively central group member is thus defined as one who possesses information in common with all or most group members. By contrast, other group members are *cognitively peripheral*; their own information is uniquely held. What they know is known by no one else, and what they may know might be really important.

For that very reason, well-functioning groups need to take advantage of cognitively peripheral people. These people are especially significant. But in most groups, cognitively central people have a disproportionate influence in discussion and participate more in group deliberations. By contrast, cognitively peripheral people end up having little influence and participate less, often to the group's detriment.

A simple explanation for these results is that group members *prefer* to hear information that is commonly held—and prefer to hear people who have such information. Cognitively central people also have high levels of credibility, while cognitively peripheral people have correspondingly low levels. And in the particular experiment just described, the executives who were cognitively central ended up having a greater influence on the final judgments. The general conclusion is that when some group members count more than others, it is often because members to whom people most listen know only what everyone else knows. Unfortunately, people who are more peripheral, with unique knowledge, are often the ones group members most need to hear.

As might be expected, a group's focus on shared information increases with the size of the group.[18] For this reason, groups can go badly wrong even if they are fairly large, and would seem to be well informed—a real problem for the wisdom of crowds. In a study designed to test judgments about candidates for office, involving both three-person and six-person groups, all the group discussions focused far more on shared information than on unshared information—but the effect was significantly greater for six-person groups. Most remarkably, the researchers reported, "it was almost as likely for a shared item to be mentioned twice as it was for an unshared item to be mentioned at all."[19]

It follows that for very large groups—twelve people, thirty people, two hundred people—the effect of shared information will be compounded. And despite the failures of their deliberations, group members tend to be significantly more confident about their judgments after discussion—and we have seen that confidence and error are a bad combination.

Why Hidden Profiles?

Why do hidden profiles remain hidden? The principal explanations build on the informational and social influence accounts emphasized thus far. When information is held by all or most group members, it is especially likely, as a statistical matter, to be repeated in group discussion and hence more likely to be influential than information that is held by one person or a few people. There are two points here. First, shared information, simply because it is shared, is more likely to be mentioned and explored during group discussion. Second, information held by all or most group members is more likely to influence individual judgments, and those judgments will in turn affect the judgments of the group.

Suppose that a team of five people is advising the president whether to embark on military action to combat a perceived threat. If each of the five people has information indicating that the use of military force would be successful, that information is likely to be discussed by the group—far more so than are separate parcels of information, individually held by each adviser, suggesting that the use of force would run into trouble. If the team of advisers stresses the information that is held in advance by each, that information will have a disproportionate influence on its ultimate decision. This is a simple statistical point.

But hidden profiles remain a lot more hidden than would be predicted by statistics alone. To understand the additional element, consider the finding that low-status members of groups are "increasingly reluctant over the course of discussion to repeat unique information."[20] Those in the group who are inexperienced or are thought to be low in the hierarchy are particularly loath to emphasize their privately held information as discussion proceeds. In a business, then, leaders are unlikely to receive the views of those who do not have much experience or respect, even if these less powerful people know something important. The same can happen in the White House and in the boardroom at General Motors.

This important finding suggests that group members, and especially lower-status ones, are nervous about emphasizing information that most group members lack. Indeed, lower-status members might well shut up. They do so partly because of the difficulty of establishing the credibility and relevance of the information they have, and partly because they risk the group's disapproval if they press a line of argument that others reject. We have seen that cognitively peripheral members have little influence on the group. Those who have uniquely held information end up participating less than those who have shared information, and what the cognitively peripheral members have to say is undervalued. In many deliberating groups, people who emphasize uniquely held information take an obvious social risk. Unfortunately for the group, they understand this risk.

Hidden profiles thus create a big problem for many groups, which fail to get information that they need and are therefore led to error. Group members typically underestimate the performance of low-status members and typically overestimate the performance of high-status members, in a way that gives high-status members a degree of deference that is not warranted by reality.[21]

Liking

Here is related problem. Those who discuss shared information tend to get a nice social reward: after a group member discusses shared information, other group members end up thinking that he or she is more competent and likable. Maybe that finding is not so surprising. It may be built into human nature to respect and like people more once they have told you something that you already know. ("If they tell me that, they must be smart, and nice too!") But perhaps more surprisingly, and certainly more tellingly, a person who is provided with information that she already has ends up feeling more competent and likable in her own eyes as well.[22] Strange but true (and important): if someone tells you something you already know, you will probably like not only that person, but also yourself, a bit better as a result. ("If they tell me that, I must be smart, and nice too!")

In face-to-face discussions and in purely written exchanges, people give higher ratings (in terms of knowledge, competence, and credibility) both to themselves and to others after receiving information that they knew already. This finding is full of implications. Within groups, those who reject the apparent consensus risk their own reputation along important dimensions. They also endanger their own self-image. It is no wonder, in this light, that common knowledge is emphasized and that people self-censor even when they could reveal a hidden profile.

Here's a suggestion: suppose that you have valuable but unshared information. You may do best to earn credibility and trust first. You can do that "by telling others what they already know before telling them what they do not already know."[23] That strategy might work, helping to furnish information that could steer groups in the right directions.

A Very Quick Recap of Part 1

Our goal in part 1 has been to catalog four common failures of deliberating groups. (1) Sometimes individual errors are amplified, not merely propagated, as a result of deliberation. (2) Groups fall victim to cascade effects, as the early speakers or actors ensure that people do not learn what is known by their successors. (3) Because of group polarization, members of deliberating groups often end up in a more extreme position in line with their predeliberation tendencies. (4) In deliberating groups, shared information often dominates or crowds out unshared information, ensuring that groups do not learn everything that their members know.

We have seen that informational signals and reputational pressure help to explain all four errors. A disturbing result is that groups often do not improve on, and sometimes do worse than, their average or median member. For many deliberating groups, a crucially important task is to devise strategies that will overcome these problems and increase the likelihood that group judgments will take advantage of the knowledge held by group members or perhaps by those who are not in the group at all. How can that be done?

Let's answer that question.

PART 2

How Groups Succeed

6

Eight Ways to Reduce Failures

Imagine that a group's leader believes that a lot of group members have valuable information and perspectives, and she wants to elicit their ideas. What can she do?

Most managers are exceedingly busy, confronting a daunting number of tasks. It is tempting for them to prefer employees who offer upbeat projections and whose essential message is that there is no need to worry. Employees are well aware of that temptation, and many of them are reluctant to provide their bosses with bad news. No one likes to be anxious or spread anxiety, especially to those who have power over them.

We have seen that in the Obama administration, Nancy-Ann DeParle and Jeff Zients solved that problem by making it clear that they wanted to hear the truth, even if it consisted of bad news. If they didn't get it, they would ask questions until they did. All over the world, wise groups benefit from the same practice.

By the way, we do not want to be viewed as opposed to optimism. Optimistic emotions and positive energy are enormously valuable, *in their place*. Optimistic people might well be more likely to succeed. But we see no role for unrealistic optimism in the early stages of an endeavor, when options are being evaluated and plans are being made. The time for optimism is *after the decision has been made*, when unified commitment to the course of action becomes essential and where even somewhat unrealistic aspirations can motivate the hard work and perseverance that are necessary for the highest levels of achievement.

One of our central themes is the immense importance of *diversity*, not necessarily along demographic lines, but in terms of ideas and perspectives. We are speaking above all of cognitive diversity. One of the virtues of anxiety is that it tends to reflect and to produce such diversity. In addition, leaders can do a great deal to increase diversity, both by creating the right kind of culture and by hiring the right kind of people.

One of the particular advantages of diversity and dissent is that they promote two things that institutions need: creativity and innovation.[1] When minority voices are heard, well-functioning groups are likely to be jolted out of their routines, and fresh solutions, even a high degree of innovation, can follow. When dissent and diversity are present and levels of participation are high, groups are likely to do a lot better.[2]

It is important to understand just how to harness the power of diversity. Many groups mistakenly mix together into one process both divergent functions, which require diverse views, *and* consensus-seeking, critical functions. It is important to think ahead to understand when each objective is needed and to plan the group process to achieve each objective separately, even to the degree of insulating the two processes from one another by designing a two-stage strategy. Interestingly, this insight is supported by conceptual arguments from Darwinian evolutionary theory and from the modern computer science of machine learning (more on this important distinction in chapter 7). For now, keep in mind that both divergent and consensus processes are needed, but are best when implemented in separate stages of the larger problem-solving strategy.

In line with our pleas for anxious leadership and for diversity, we suggest eight potential approaches: (1) inquisitive and self-silencing leaders; (2) "priming" critical thinking; (3) rewarding group success; (4) role assignment; (5) perspective changing; (6) devil's advocates; (7) red teams; and (8) the Delphi method. We begin with the simplest and least formal and move toward approaches that have a higher degree of complexity and structure.

Inquisitive and Self-Silencing Leaders

Even if they have important information, some people are more likely to silence themselves than others. We have noted that group members are more likely to speak out if they have high social status or are confident about their own views.[3] We have also referred to the complementary finding that members of low-status groups—less educated people, African Americans, and sometimes women—may have less influence within deliberating groups.[4] On juries, lower-status members, as measured by their occupations and sex, have been found to be less active and less influential in deliberation.[5] Not surprisingly, one of the greatest studies of the jury process, *The American Jury*, surveyed judges and juries in the early 1960s and found that men out-talked women two-to-one in jury deliberations.[6] But we were surprised when forty years later, analyzing our own jury deliberation data, we found that men still out-talked women two-to-one in jury deliberations. In many companies, a similar situation undoubtedly holds.

Wise groups take careful account of these findings and take corrective steps. Revealingly, the risk that unshared information will have too little influence is much reduced when that information is held by a leader within a group. Not surprisingly, leaders are eager to share the information that they have. And the leaders' words usually count, because people listen to what leaders have to say.[7]

Consider a revealing experiment. A medical team consisting of a resident physician, an intern, and a third-year medical student was asked to diagnose an illness. The team displayed a strong tendency to emphasize unshared items stressed by the *resident*, who was the highest-status member of the group. In this particular respect, the team did not fall prey to the problem of hidden profiles—because the resident's information, even though uniquely held, was successfully transmitted to all group members.[8] More generally, people who are experienced in the task at hand are more likely to mention and to repeat unshared information.

One reason for these findings is that those with higher status or competence are less subject to the social pressures that lead people to silence themselves. Another reason is that leaders and experts are more likely to think that their own information is most important and worth disclosing to the group—notwithstanding the fact that the information held by other group members cuts in the other direction.

The simplest lesson is that leaders and high-status members can do the group a big service by indicating their willingness and their desire to *hear* uniquely held information. If they are inquisitive, they are more likely to learn. Of course, time is scarce, but quick meetings in which leaders ask for information that has not yet emerged can be a big help. (In government, Sunstein created a "fifteen-minute rule," meaning that staff meetings could not go over fifteen minutes unless there was special reason—and the short time ensured that a lot of information flooded the group from the start.) Leaders can also refuse to state a firm view at the outset and in that way allow space for more information to emerge.

"Priming" Critical Thinking

We have seen that when people silence themselves in deliberating groups, it is often because of social norms—because of a sense that their reputations will suffer and that they will be punished, not rewarded, for disclosing information that departs from their group's inclination. Hidden profiles remain hidden in large part for this reason; those who disclose unique information face a risk of disapproval.

But none of this is inevitable. Social norms are not set in stone. If consensus is prized and known to be prized, then self-silencing will be more likely. But if the group is known to welcome new and competing information, then the reward structure will be fundamentally different and will support much better outcomes.

Social scientists have done a lot of work on the importance of *priming*—that is, triggering some association or thought in such a way as to affect people's choices and behavior. If male teachers and female students are primed to think of gender, they act differently, more in conformity with gender stereotypes. Words like *Wall Street* increase people's propensity to compete and reduce the chances they will cooperate. In one study, if the participants thought that the name of the game they were asked to play was *Community Game*, they were far more likely to work together than if they thought the name was the *Wall Street Game*.[9]

Self-silencing can be affected by priming as well. Striking evidence for this claim comes from hidden-profile experiments that prime people by asking them to engage in a prior task that involved either "getting along" or, instead, "critical thinking."[10] When the prime involved getting along, people sensed that their goal was to cooperate and to be friendly with one another. When the prime involved critical thinking, people felt that their goal was to arrive at the right solution. Once people were primed by a task that called for critical thinking, they were far more likely to disclose what they knew—and there was a substantial reduction of hidden profiles. Good team players think critically, and they do not always get along. Wise groups can prime that particular action.

This point applies to many organizations, including corporate boards. In the United States, the highest-performing companies tend to have "extremely contentious boards that regard dissent as an obligation" and that "have a good fight now and then."[11] Recall that unsuccessful investment clubs have little dissent and lose a great deal of money when the members are united by close social ties. By contrast, the best-performing investment clubs lack such ties and benefit from dissent and diversity.[12]

For both private and public groups, the general lesson is clear. If the group encourages disclosure of information—even if the information opposes the group's inclination—then self-silencing will be reduced significantly. Deliberation will benefit as a result. Good social norms and a good culture can go a long way toward reducing the potentially bad effects of social pressures. Although there is no simple or automatic way to encourage disclosure, leadership makes a big difference and leaders can inculcate norms that help. Subtle pressures toward conformity can be avoided. Genuine (rather than merely symbolic) openness to different or disagreeable views, sometimes in the form of material rewards, matters a lot. Happy talk can be rewarded—or it can be countered with some version of, "OK, now tell me something I need to know."

Rewarding Group Success

We have seen that people often silence themselves because they receive only a fraction of the benefits of disclosure. This point raises an obvious question: How would groups perform if individuals knew that they would be rewarded not if their own answer was correct, but if *the majority of the group* turns out to be correct?

In a situation of this kind, hidden profiles, cascades, and group polarization will be reduced. If people are rewarded when their group is right, they are far more likely to reveal what they actually know. In such a situation, incentives are changed, because people internalize the benefits of disclosure. Good managers are entirely aware of that fact.

Careful experiments show that it is possible to restructure incentives in just this way—and hence to reduce the likelihood of cascades.[13] Cascades are far less likely when each individual knows that he has nothing to gain from a correct *individual* decision and everything to gain from a correct *group* decision. Groups produce much better outcomes when it is in the individual's interest to report exactly what he sees or knows. It is the candid and fully informative announcement, from each person, that is most likely to promote an accurate group decision.

An emphasis on the importance of group success can improve decisions in many real-world contexts, simply because the emphasis provides better access to more minds. Consider the case of whistle-blowing—a practice understood not merely as disclosing inappropriate or unlawful conduct, but more broadly as drawing attention to possible flaws in the group's plans and actions. Whistle-blowing is often a product not of the whistle-blower's narrow self-interest, but of the whistle-blower's desire to ensure that the organization or group succeeds.

True, some whistle-blowers are malcontents, but many of them are sincerely trying to promote their group's success rather than their own. In poorly functioning groups, whistle-blowers act at their own risk, which makes it less likely that people will become whistle-blowers at all. Wise groups welcome some whistle-blowing. Loyalty is important, but when people reveal information aimed to make a group work better, they are hardly being disloyal.

The general lesson is that identification with the group's success is more likely to ensure that people will say what they know, regardless of whether it fits the party line. And if group members focus on their own personal prospects rather than those of the group, the group is more likely to err. Both social norms and material incentives can play crucial roles in establishing the priorities of group members. The challenge is to introduce one or the other, or both, into deliberating groups.

The Role of Roles

Experimental Evidence

Imagine a deliberating group consisting of people with specific roles that are appreciated and known by all group members. One person might have medical expertise; another might be a lawyer; a third might know about public relations; a fourth might be a statistician. In such a group, sensible information aggregation should be far more likely, simply because each member knows, in advance, that each of the others has something to contribute. Hidden profiles will be less likely to remain hidden if there is a division of labor, in which each person is known to be knowledgeable about something in particular.[14] Specialists can be helpful, not only because of their specialized knowledge, but also because they will feel empowered to speak up.

Several experiments strongly support the hypothesis.[15] In one such experiment, each member of a three-person group was given a good deal of independent information about one of three murder suspects.[16] In half of these groups, the specific "expertise" of each member was publicly identified to everyone before discussion began. In the other half, there was no such public identification of the specialists. The bias in favor of shared information was much reduced in the groups with the publicly identified experts; the public identification operated as an effective device to solve the information-sharing problem. By contrast, the reduction of the bias was a lot smaller when experts were not identified publicly and when each group member was only privately told, by the experimenter, that he or she was an expert on a particular candidate.

The lesson is clear. If a group wants to obtain the information that its members hold, all group members should be told, before deliberation begins, that different members have different, and relevant, information to contribute. The effect of role assignment in reducing hidden profiles can be significant in solving the challenges of eliciting distributed information.

Diverse "Equities"

Let's turn from behavioral lab experiments to the real world. As Sunstein observed up close, a strong form of role assignment occurs in the federal government. When the process works well, it makes government groups very wise. The EPA has many employees who know a lot about clean air and clean water. Those at the US Department of Agriculture are experts on farming and agriculture. The Department of Transportation knows about highways and railroads. The Department of State and the Office of the US Trade Representative are concerned with international relationships, and they know about the effects of American policies on other nations and on US relationships with these nations.

In his role as administrator of OIRA, Sunstein frequently saw good decisions emerge from processes in which every agency's role, with its distinctive expertise and perspective, was respected. In fact, part of Sunstein's job was to make sure that those involved in making decisions listened to different people, with their different roles. When the system worked well, there were no hidden profiles and people did not become polarized or join cascades.

In government, people commonly speak of the *equities* of various participants in discussions. It's an ugly term, to be sure, but a daily part of government-speak. (While we are at it, other awful terms include *do-out*, for tasks that follow meetings; *deliverables*, for products of work; *loop in*, meaning to include someone; and *circle back*, for getting back to someone. Ugh, to be sure.) The word *equities* is a shorthand way to signal that diverse people's views and roles matter and require independent attention, concern, and respect.

For those who work in government, talk of equities can be frustrating and even infuriating. Those who engage in such talk can be obstacles to the effort to obtain consensus, and a consensus is often necessary to get anything done. What's worse, the term suggests that participants ought to focus not on what is right, but on the arguments and concerns that grow out of their distinctive positions. But when the process is working well, the idea of equities is indispensable. It licenses people to provide information and perspectives that reflect their own role—and thus ensures that important information doesn't get lost. Even if a leader isn't especially wise about information pooling, participation by people with diverse equities can ensure that the group learns what it needs to know.

One reason that government sometimes decides badly is that diverse people do not end up in the most important rooms. The simple lesson: leaders in both private and public sectors do well when they ensure that people are assigned different tasks and roles.

Perspective Changing

Here's a useful tactic, one that applies a version of the idea of role assignment. Suppose that you are a leader of an organization and that it is not doing well, perhaps because it is stuck in old ways of thinking. Recall that even more than individuals, groups stick to courses of action that are failing. What can you do?

Intel Corporation, a large American company, faced exactly this problem in the 1980s. After fourteen years of profits, it was losing a lot of business in the memory chip market, which it had pioneered. In a dramatic move, the company decided to abandon the entire market.[17] Its CEO, Andrew Grove, explained the decision:

> *I remember a time in the middle of 1985, after this aimless wandering had been going on for almost a year. I was in my office with Intel's chairman and CEO, Gordon Moore, and we were discussing our quandary. Our mood was downbeat. I looked out the window at the Ferris wheel of the Great America amusement park revolving in the distance, then I turned back to Gordon and I asked, "If we got kicked out and the board brought in a new CEO, what do you think he would do?" Gordon answered without hesitation, "He would get us out of memories." I stared at him, numb, then said, "Why shouldn't you and I walk out the door, come back and do it ourselves?"*[18]

This is a profound story, because Grove was able to shock himself out of his routine thought processes by a purely hypothetical role assignment, in which he asked Moore, and himself, what a new CEO would do. That question changed his perspective by creating a critical distance. For Intel, it initiated a spectacularly successful new strategy. The story suggests that when a group is aimlessly wandering or on a path that does not seem so good, it is an excellent idea to ask, "If we brought in new leadership, what would it do?" Asking that simple question can break through a host of conceptual traps.

Speak of the Devil

If hidden profiles and self-silencing are the source of group failure, then an obvious response is to ask some group members to act as devil's advocates, deliberately advocating a position that is contrary to the group's inclination. Throughout recent history, both public and private sectors have shown a lot of interest in devil's advocacy. The basic idea was a central suggestion of both the 2005 Senate committee reporting on intelligence failures in connection with the Iraq War and the 2007 review board that investigated a series of blunders at the National Aeronautics and Space Administration (NASA).

Some successful leaders show an implicit awareness of the importance of listening to devils. Such leaders try to elicit diverse views not through any kind of formal process, but by indicating their own agreement with different (and incompatible) positions. Consider the distinctive practice of President Franklin Delano Roosevelt, who sometimes took the ingenious approach of indicating his agreement with people having inconsistent positions. All the advisers thought that the president agreed with them, so they were emboldened to develop and elaborate their diverging opinions.

Roosevelt's approach gave people the confidence and license to produce the best arguments on behalf of their positions. When

Roosevelt made up his mind, it was only after he heard a sincere and rigorous statement of conflicting positions, offered by people who believed, firmly if erroneously, that the president shared their views. No doubt, his advisers sometimes were upset when they finally learned what he really thought.

Roosevelt's practice was a good one, because in any White House, presidential advisers are greatly tempted to silence their doubts and to provide a unified and supportive front. To say the least, the president is busy, and he has the weight of the world on his shoulders; many advisers do not want to trouble him or to create internal disagreement. They also want the president to like and approve of them, and those who challenge the president's view, or the views of other advisers, risk incurring disapproval. For this reason, some White House advisers have a tendency to offer happy talk to the president. This practice can avoid conflict and unpleasantness, but is not in the interest of the president, the nation, or the world. Of course, the president is unique, but something analogous can be said about the boss at many organizations.

The idea of the devil's advocate is meant to formalize the commitment to the expression of dissenting viewpoints. In at least one well-known case, the approach appeared to work. As Irving Janis described, "during the Cuban missile crisis, President Kennedy gave his brother, the Attorney General, the unambiguous mission of playing devil's advocate, with seemingly excellent results in breaking up a premature consensus"—a consensus that might well have led to war.[19] It is worthwhile to wonder whether and when similar assignments might have proved helpful with the presidents who followed Kennedy.

By their very nature, those assuming the role of devil's advocate are able to avoid the social pressure that comes from rejecting the dominant position within the group. After all, they are charged with doing precisely that. And because they are specifically asked to take a contrary position, they are freed from the informational influences that can lead to self-silencing.

Hidden profiles are a lot less likely to remain hidden if a devil's advocate is directed to disclose the information she has, even if that information runs contrary to the apparent consensus within the group. In groups that are at risk of hidden profiles, a devil's advocate should help a great deal. For groups that seek to get wiser, it would seem sensible to appoint devil's advocates.

So much for theory. Unfortunately, we cannot give a strong endorsement of this approach, because research on devil's advocacy in small groups provides mixed support. True, there is some evidence for the view that devil's advocates can be helpful.[20] Many experiments do find that genuine dissenting views can enhance group performance.[21]

But there is a difference between authentic dissent and a formal requirement of devil's advocacy; an assigned devil's advocate does far less to improve group performance. One reason is that any such requirement is artificial—a kind of exercise or game—and group members are aware of that fact. The devil's advocate can seem to be just going through the motions. And indeed, when an advocate's challenges to a group consensus are insincere, group members discount the arguments accordingly. At best, the devil's advocate facilitates a more sophisticated inquiry into the problem at hand.[22]

Because arbitrarily selected devil's advocates are acting out a role and have no real incentive to sway the group's members to their side, they succeed in their assigned role even if they allow the consensus view to refute their unpopular arguments. Unlike a genuine dissenter, the devil's advocate has little to gain by zealously challenging the dominant view—and as a result such advocates often fail to vigorously challenge the consensus.[23]

The lesson is that if devil's advocacy is to work, it will be because the dissenter actually means what she is saying. If so, better decisions should be expected. If not, the exercise will turn out to be a mere formality, with little corrective power. Considering the existing evidence, we suggest that it is a lot better for groups to encourage real dissent—by, for example, assigning roles to experts representing different knowledge sets or perspectives—than to appoint formal, artificial dissenters. Designating groups of dissenters composed of members who, before deliberation, sincerely favor different solutions can solve some hidden-profile problems.[24]

Contrarian Teams

Another method, related to the appointment of a devil's advocate but more effective according to existing research, is called *red teaming*. This method has been extensively applied to military teamwork, but it can be applied in a lot of domains, including business and government.[25] Any implementation plan, if it has a high level of ambition, might benefit from red teaming.

Red teaming involves the creation of a team that is given the task of criticizing or defeating a primary team's plans to execute a mission. There are two basic forms of red teams: those that play an adversary role and attempt to defeat the primary team in a simulated mission, and those given the same instructions as a devil's advocate, which is to construct the strongest case against a proposal or plan. Even an artificial role assignment can be powerful enough to produce substantial improvements, if the assignment is to more than one dissenter. It is as if having more than one dissenter provides social proof of the validity or at least the significance of the divergent views. Anxious people can also operate as the functional equivalent of red teams, and sometimes they enlist red teams to test worst-case scenarios.

Versions of this method are used in all branches of the military and in many government offices. (Important government regulations are sometimes evaluated with the help of informal red teams.) In industry, some firms offer red-teaming services to other companies, as in the case of "white-hat hackers" who are paid to attempt to subvert software security systems and to penetrate corporate firewalls.

Within law firms, there has been a long tradition of pretrials, or the testing of arguments with the equivalent of red teams. In important cases, such efforts can reach the level of hiring attorneys from a second firm to develop and present a case against advocates from the primary firm. Often these adversarial tests are conducted before mock juries so that the success of the primary and red-team arguments can be evaluated through the eyes of citizens similar to those who will render the ultimate courtroom verdict.

One size does not fit all, and the cost and feasibility of red teams will vary from one organization to another. But in many contexts, red teams are an excellent idea, especially if they are sincerely motivated to find mistakes and to exploit vulnerabilities and are given clear incentives to do exactly that.

The Delphi Method

Is there a way to obtain the benefits of individually held information while also supporting the kinds of learning that deliberation is designed to promote? To overcome social influences, leaders might simply ask people to state their opinions anonymously and independently, maybe before deliberation, so that their private statements are available to others. The secret ballot can be understood as an effort to insulate people from social pressures and to permit them to say what they actually believe. Some groups should consider more routine use of the preliminary secret ballot, simply to elicit more information. The challenge is then to answer this question: What should groups do with the votes that emerge from secret ballots?

As an ambitious effort to answer that question, consider the Delphi method, a formal process for aggregating the views of group members. The Delphi method, which can be undertaken via computer networks or in a traditional meeting, has several key features.[26] In many of its applications, the method is simply a version of averaging that enlists social learning.

Here's how it works. Individuals offer first-round estimates (or votes) in complete anonymity. Then a cycle of reestimations (or repeated voting) occurs, with a statistical requirement that forces convergence; the second-round individual votes have to fall within the middle quartiles (25–75 percent) of the range of the first round's estimates. This process is repeated until group members converge on a single point estimate. Although this is essentially a social averaging process, people need not converge on the mathematical average or median, as individuals can use the distributions of prior estimates from their colleagues to inform their new votes. This process allows, for example, a very confident (or stubborn) voter to exert more weight on the final outcome than in a numerical calculation.

The Delphi method has a quirky history, having been invented at the RAND Corporation to assist military and diplomatic analysis of cold war scenarios. Originally it was applied to forecast military-technological developments and to anticipate the actions of an opponent in a strategic diplomatic negotiation or war. Like many RAND inventions, its applications have shifted to peacetime questions, usually concerned with forecasting events from politics (e.g., regime shifts, election outcomes) and industry (e.g., sales volumes, unemployment rates). In some recent applications, the method has been used to promote information sharing, rather than forcing consensus on estimates or solutions. In one application, over one thousand contributions were solicited with respect to the creation of a proposal for the development of international web-based communication systems in Central and South America.[27]

The Delphi method has some significant virtues. First, it ensures the initial anonymity of all members through a purely private statement of views. The purpose of anonymity is precisely "to diminish the effects of social pressures, as from vocally dominant or dogmatic individuals, or from a majority."[28] Second, people are given an opportunity to offer feedback on one another's views. Group members are permitted to communicate—sometimes fully, but sometimes only their ultimate conclusions. The conclusions, given anonymously, are always provided to others by a facilitator, sometimes in the form of a statistical summary or a tabulation (histogram) of all the responses. Thus "the feedback comprises the opinions and judgments of all group members and not just the most vocal."[29] Finally, and after the relevant communication, the judgments of group members are elicited again and subject to another statistical aggregation.

In several contexts, the Delphi method has worked well.[30] For general-knowledge questions, the method yielded better answers than did individual estimates—though open discussion did still better, apparently because it served to correct errors.[31] Note here that the Delphi method is more successful when group members are provided not only with the mean or median estimate, but also with the *reasons* that group members have for their views.[32] An account of reasons is most likely to move people in the direction of the correct answer.[33] New technologies can easily be enlisted in the use of the Delphi method.

In one experiment, people were asked to consider specified heights and weights and to say whether people with those heights and weights are more likely to be male or female.[34] Deliberating groups did no better than statistical groups on that task; often, deliberating groups did worse. (Recall from chapter 1 that a statistical group is one whose members do not confer with another before they make a decision; instead the members' solutions are combined objectively, usually with a mathematical equation.) But the authors tried a third method of aggregating opinions, one close to the Delphi method. Under that method, people were asked to make private estimates initially. After a period of discussion, people were then asked to make final estimates. These were the most successful groups. A simple approach of estimate-talk-estimate radically reduced errors.

A natural alternative to the Delphi method would be a system in which ultimate judgments are stated anonymously, but only after deliberation. Anonymity, both in advance and at the conclusion, would insulate group members from reputational pressure and, to that extent, could reduce the problem of self-silencing. Wise groups should be experimenting with the Delphi method or at least with less formal variations. Such groups need not worry over close adherence to the particulars of the Delphi method; they can act more informally to combine a degree of initial anonymity with some room for discussion.

We have covered a number of approaches here, from the relatively simple to the more formalized. The evidence suggests that all of them can make groups wiser. Managers should not be pests, but they can jerk people out of complacency and encourage the group to spend some time on worst-case scenarios. All of our approaches can be seen as efforts to make groups a bit less cheerful. In our own experience, role assignment has particular promise and should be used far more widely than it now is, certainly if the assignment is designed not as part of a game, but as a serious endeavor.

Playing Moneyball

We have referred to Michael Lewis's *Moneyball*, which demonstrated that statistical analysis outperforms judgments made on the basis of intuition, anecdotes, and experience. Our emphasis in this chapter has been on how to improve group performance, but we offer a final note, which involves the importance of relying on data and evidence whenever you can. Within the federal government, cost-benefit analysis has become the coin of the realm and is an important corrective to individual and group errors. If you can obtain and analyze data, you can often overcome most of the problems we have identified, because many of our problems are based on losing contact with reality. Nothing seems to inject reality into a discussion and banish wishful thinking and biased speculations as well as empirical evidence, especially in the form of data and numbers.

7

A Framework for Improvement

Identifying and Selecting Solutions

On some occasions, a decision-making or problem-solving process demands critical thinking—winnowing out the chaff and zeroing in on the nuggets of good solutions. But on other occasions, it requires a more creative, less critical, more open-ended approach. Over the years that we have been involved in collective endeavors and immersed in the relevant behavioral findings, we have concluded that breaking down the process into two stages provides valuable insights on how to enhance group work. We have briefly referred to this point earlier; it is now time to offer more details about how to separate, implement, and optimize the divergent and convergent stages of every problem-solving process.

In some cases, the group begins with a set of possible solutions, and the remaining task is to select the best solution from that set. But often, groups have to solve a more complex problem. In such cases, the *identification of potential solutions* is the most important challenge that the group faces; the group must find and catalog those solutions before it can select the best one. In practice, it is often best to separate those two stages, identification and selection, of the larger process. Furthermore, the conditions that enhance each of the two stages are different. Effective process design depends on knowing when to execute each stage and how to provide for the different conditions that optimize each.

Much of what we have said bears on innovation and search, and not only on selection of the best solution. For example, the use of both red teams and role assignments can flush out solutions that a group initially neglected, as well as help in the evaluation and selection of decisions that have been identified. In this chapter, we make a sharp distinction between the identification and the selection of solutions, and we explore how groups should deal differently with the two tasks.

The Distinction between Identification and Selection

The two-stage identification and selection process goes under many names. It is the essential mechanism of Darwinian evolution in biology; philosophers refer to it as universal Darwinism or evolutionary epistemology; and psychologists talk of trial-and-error learning.[1] These labels all refer to the same general two-stage process, perhaps clearest in its original evolutionary context. In the evolution of species, organisms are created with some variation that is introduced by genetic recombination and mutation mechanisms during reproduction. Then the environment selects the organisms that are the fittest. These "solutions," the fittest organisms, are passed on to the next generation through their genetic code. Then this cycle is repeated generation after generation. Eventually, after the two-stage process—the generation (we call this *"identification"* in our discussion of group processes) of new organisms and then the *selection* of the fittest from the new generation—has repeated many times, evolution has "selected out" the organisms that are unfit for the environment. The result is "adapted," often close-to-optimal organisms.

The identification and selection process is also the essential mechanism in the field of machine learning in modern computer science, where the process is called the *genetic algorithm.*[2] When complex learning needs to occur—suppose a program has been written to search a complex mathematical space for the solution to an equation—a basic template for a solution is set up and the program randomly tries various values. When the values generated by the random process are closer to the objectives defined for the problem, the elements of that approximate solution are rescrambled and then tested again. Solutions that are closer to the objectives are retained and rescrambled; solutions that fail are thrown away. This cycle of *identification* (by scrambling prior good solutions) and *selection* continues for thousands of trials (generations) until a good solution is found. Explorations of how to refine this identification and selection process are among the major research programs in computer science today. This same genetic algorithm machine learning approach is used in many of the breakthrough data-mining applications to find patterns in large data sets.

These same ideas are essential in psychological theories of individual creativity and concept learning. They are applied in a practical form in the methods that are used every day at IDEO, Eureka! Ranch, and many other companies that sell innovation processes to other companies.[3] The recipe for innovation, used by these companies, is this same two-stage process: brainstorm to generate new solutions, then critically evaluate to select the best solutions from those identified in the first stage.

Decision-making groups do not have the time to run thousands of machine learning simulations or thousands of biological generations, but they can cycle through the two-stage identification and selection process once, twice, or three times. If conditions are favorable, even a single pass through the two separate stages produces collective solutions that are better than what can be achieved by the best individual solvers or deciders.

The identification stage focuses on the problem of generating many alternative solutions, without giving any of them a time-consuming and inhibiting evaluation. The identification stage can involve a *search* for solutions to add to the consideration set of possible solutions. (A company that makes computer games searches for a cutting-edge virtual reality system and acquires the company that manufactures it.) Alternatively, it could rely on *refinement* of a current design or the integration of several successful current designs. (The Apple iPhone is an elegant combination of the features of many precursor cell phones, each tweaked to the next level of refinement and then integrated into a dominant product.) Finally, the stage can pursue *invention* methods to create new solutions. (An appliance manufacturer spends hundreds of millions of dollars to reengineer the electrical motor in its products, inventing a new engine that is more powerful, weighs one-tenth as much, and operates on a magnetic pulsing principle, rather than rotating metal brushes.) For almost any problem-solving system, it is better to separate selection, with its emphasis on critical evaluations, from identification, which is best served by an uncritical, open-minded attitude. The qualities of a good selection process—critical, anxious, skeptical evaluation—are antithetical to the qualities that make for a creative, open-minded, divergent process like identification.

To introduce the conditions that make the two-stage identification and selection process work, let's imagine a company that wants to offer a new social network product. That's an ambitious idea, to be sure, and maybe preposterously so, but please bear with us for a bit.

How can the group solve the first problem of identifying possible networking website solutions that will be evaluated in the second selection stage? There are many examples of social networking sites out there on the internet, and a good start for the identification stage is to search for existing solutions. A quick search finds many sites: Myspace, Facebook, Google+, LinkedIn, Twitter, Meetup, VK, Pinterest.

For some companies, an existing website might be the best solution. If the company has the resources, it can identify an existing solution and then acquire it. We see this happening every day in the business news, as Google, Facebook, Microsoft, and IBM snap up smaller innovative firms. For the company in our example, the identification stage would simply need to uncover as many suitable candidate sites as possible. These would be passed on to the selection stage and scrutinized, with reference to the company's criteria for an ideal site. Then the best already-existing site in the set of candidates would be identified and acquired.

If search is the method used to solve the identification stage, it is important that the search be broad and inclusive. You achieve breadth and inclusiveness by using many independent clues or by searching in many directions over a wide landscape of potential solutions. Many searches, independent searchers, and diverse searches are all good characteristics of a process aimed to solve the identification stage.

A second approach in the identification stage would be to *refine or redesign* a current site. This might mean imitating current sites, perhaps with modifications, minor or not so minor, that would produce innovative solutions. This method of finding existing good solutions and then refining them or mixing up the parts of a few of those solutions is the essence of one approach to creativity. For example, *Why Not?*—an insightful book on enhancing individual creativity—is focused on the use of analogies and transfers of a solution from one setting to another.[4]

If a television show is successful in Denmark, consider an American version of the same story. If a mechanism works to save money in European hotels, implement it in American motels. For our hypothetical project, consider LinkedIn. This popular (if also irritating!) networking site for workers and professionals serves career development and employee recruiting needs for its users. The invention process might consider a variation on the original website that provides networking for a specialized occupation—maybe a career networking site serving professional athletes. The site could provide special features, tuned to the needs of that profession: validation of the performance records of those seeking sponsors, contact information for sponsors seeking new athletes, coaches and training centers seeking students, and so forth.

A third approach to identification would be to *invent* a new solution that has not been exploited by any other sites. For example, families are the most essential human social group. So how about a site that links family members, provides family-oriented archives (photo albums, recipe files, biographies, medical records) and services (genealogy analysis, wedding planning), and attracts new members by finding connections through biological kinship links?

Sure, many of the initial solutions will be harebrained and easy to reject at first glance. Others will be rejected because they are good solutions to some problems, but not to the problem the company is trying to solve now. But if the initial identification process is productive, there will be viable, maybe even close-to-optimal solutions in the consideration set. The important characteristic of the identification phase is that it generates many relevant solutions.

These solutions then enter the selection stage of the process. During selection, members critically evaluate the solutions to select the best one. Group members usually begin this stage by reviewing the criteria that define a good solution. As noted, many of the candidates from the identification phase will be easily rejected, but every so often, there will be a surprise, in which a nonobvious solution turns out to be the fittest, or best.

To return to our example, perhaps our fictional company is looking for a strategy that would help attract Facebook users away from that dominant site. Perhaps after critical review the family-oriented website emerges as the most promising solution. Such a website might aim at the demographic that is least active on Facebook—parents and grandparents. And it might attract younger Facebook users as they age into their parental roles and become more interested in family-oriented social links. Remember, we do not think that we have invented a Facebook-beater here (though, come to think of it, a family-oriented site might not be a bad tactic), but we are using the social-website problem to illustrate how the identification and selection mechanism operates.

One secret to the success of this two-stage method is to identify the criteria for a successful solution before you even begin to identify solutions. Keeping the criteria in the back of your mind during the identification stage can guide the process in subtle, unconscious ways to find or generate better candidates. And of course, having the criteria for a good solution in hand is essential in the selection stage. There is a delicate balance here. Extensive evaluation of candidate solutions during the identification stage gums up the process, but complete disregard for the criteria can produce a massive glut of worthless candidates.

Guidelines for the Two Stages of Decision Making

Innovation companies like IDEO seem to get this balance just right in face-to-face deliberating teams. They begin the process with a thorough review of the client's criteria for an exceptional solution, then they allow the criteria to fade into the background of consciousness and into the periphery of the group process while solutions are generated. In the selection stage, they return to the objectives to undertake a rigorous evaluation of the solutions identified.

The identification stage is where variety, independence, and diversity trump a systematic focus and even analytic reasoning. It should be obvious that a team with different perspectives, different knowledge bases, different skill sets—in short, a diverse team—is likely to generate a large and varied set of candidate solutions. And if search is the method to identify solutions, a broad search will be better. For identification, here are the important guidelines.

1. Start with well-defined objectives and criteria that will be applied later to evaluate solutions. As noted above, doing so will subtly prime the mind to produce relevant solutions that are not wildly outside the realm of acceptable solutions defined by the objectives.

2. Insulate identification from selection. It is important to discourage undue criticism and evaluation in the identification stage; those goals will be served later in the selection stage.

3. Start the group process (discussion, network-based pooling of information) with all individuals sharing their personal best solutions or best presolution concepts; then provide time between group deliberation episodes for individuals to reflect and create additional solutions stimulated by their own prior solutions and the ideas contributed by others.

4. Promote diverse solutions—within heads *and* between individuals—in the identification stage. In some applications, diversity is facilitated if the contributions are anonymous, thus avoiding the kinds of social influences that inhibit rigorous analysis.

5. Adopt some means of recording and remembering the solutions generated in the identification stage. Groups often do this with flip charts, Post-It-style idea icons, or electronic files. Innovation companies use visual reminders in effective ways.

For the selection phase, the guidelines look a lot different:

1. Review the criteria for an optimal solution and, if neces-
    sary, plan for concrete operational tests of the solutions
    passed on from the identification stage. In some applica-
    tions, this is best done by adding new group members to
    the process who are closer to the organization's primary
    leaders and who are distinguished by their focus on the
    team's or organization's mission and ultimate objectives. In
    other applications, the best approach might involve con-
    sulting the users of the final product of the process—for
    example, customers who would use or consume the solu-
    tions, citizens affected by a regulation, or others in touch
    with the implementation and consequences of the solution
    (see chapter 12).

2. Do not allow irrelevant social factors such as status,
    talkativeness, and likability of the sources of feedback to
    bias evaluations. Again, this can mean that an anonymous
    procedure (e.g., secret balloting) is the most effective
    process.

3. Adopt a *decisive* method of combining (independent) indi-
    vidual evaluations into an acceptable consensus.

The challenge of combining requirements 2 and 3 for the selection stage has led to some ingenious procedures. For example,
voting systems and market mechanisms are designed to be tamper-
proof (i.e., difficult to manipulate with insincere voting strategies
and resistant to bubbles and "market makers"), to protect minority
interests, and to maximize the chance that even those disenfran-
chised by the outcome of the decision will nonetheless accept it

and support its implementation.[5] Likewise, effective project review procedures provide for diverse, representative review panel membership at the same time that the actual review process is secret (and insulated from ulterior influences).

Putting the Guidelines into Practice

All this is pretty abstract. Let's look at some concrete examples.

The first involves the title of this very book. AllOurIdeas.org is a research tool that attempts to use surveys to tap crowd wisdom. It has received a lot of attention from both public and private institutions. To take just one example, the United Nations Division for Sustainable Development has used this crowd-sourcing tool to ask people what issues should be prioritized.

As AllOurIdeas works, people are presented with a pair of options and are asked to say which they prefer. For example, should the focus be on "Getting GDP Right" or instead on "Air Quality Standards Set Forth by the World Health Organization"? People decide between them. After making that decision, they are presented with another pair of options, and then another. All of these come from a larger preexisting set of options. But users can also add their own ideas, which then appear for later viewers to evaluate. Answers are ranked in terms of the probability that they will be chosen by someone who makes a choice in comparison with a random alternative.

You should be able to see that AllOurIdeas works by facilitating both identification (people can add their own ideas) and selection (people choose). In fact, Matthew Salganik, a trailblazing sociologist at Princeton who designed the site, assures us that he sought to facilitate both goals at once. For the title of this book, our publisher put in nine ideas; people who took the survey added nine more. The titles received over two thousand votes. Our ultimate choice was not on the original list. Someone added the suggestion, it ranked near the top, and we liked it. AllOurIdeas has clearly found a clever way to combine identification and selection.

The site has a lot of success stories, and they are growing over time. For example, Catholic Relief Services, a worldwide nongovernmental organization, used the site to develop new guidelines for recruitment and career development globally.

As a kind of lark and also as a test, we added another survey on AllOurIdeas.org, asking people to identify the most serious air pollution problem in the United States. Our candidates included particulate matter, benzene, arsenic, ozone, carbon dioxide, and carbon monoxide. In our view and in the view of most experts, particulate matter should probably rank at the top of the list, with carbon dioxide (the leading greenhouse gas) being a strong competitor. But the words *particulate matter* do not exactly strike evoke strong reactions, and we added *arsenic* somewhat mischievously; it is not a serious air pollutant, but no one likes the idea of arsenic in the ambient air. Over two hundred people took the survey, and to our big surprise, particulate matter was ranked first, with carbon dioxide second, and arsenic dead last. Some crowds do turn out to be wise.

Companies frequently use in-house or outsourced brainstorming methods to identify and select good solutions for current problems. Companies like IDEO and Eureka! Ranch have provided many reports of their innovation methods.[6] IDEO labels what we call the identification and selection mechanism the *innovation funnel*: the process starts broadly with open-ended, divergent thinking to generate or identify many solutions (IDEO calls this the "deep dive") and then selects good solutions, gradually zeroing in on one or two winning solutions. The process also includes a third stage in which the initial winning solutions are prototyped, polished, and integrated to produce a final implemented solution.

At IDEO, the identification stage is accomplished by following these steps: (1) meeting with the clients to review the objectives and the limitations for an ideal solution; (2) cycling through a social brainstorming process in which solutions are generated individually, shared, and then "built on" through a constructive, uncritical, social "riffing" process; and (3) keeping track of the solutions. The selection stage includes three steps as well: (1) reviewing the objectives and sometimes adding additional objective-focused members; (2) rigorously evaluating each solution, with reference to the criteria or objectives; (3) selecting winners, usually through a simple plurality voting scheme. Sometimes only higher-ranking members of the team or the client firm participate in the final evaluation and voting, namely those who are most informed and care the most about the objectives and criteria for a good solution.

In many commercial innovation procedures, there is a third stage, design implementation, in which the best solutions from the identification and selection mechanism are prototyped, tested, and refined before final implementation. Notice that many of the most highly regarded innovations from companies like Apple and Microsoft are primarily the results of only this final refining and implementation stage. In important respects, the iPod, iPhone, and iPad were all fully "invented" before these projects were taken on by Apple, where they were refined into much more user-friendly versions by Apple's design and engineering staffs.

Nothing at all to sneer at here—but the notion that Apple *created* these products is not entirely accurate. What Apple did was to select features from a universe of many similar products and then combined them and refined them into more elegant, usable objects of desire.

How Identification and Selection Processes Reduce Biases

In chapter 2, we saw many examples of how biases can undermine group performance. Fortunately, effective identification and selection processes can reduce the effects of those biases.

Some biases involve various forms of myopia—of seeking too little information or of focusing unduly on a few pieces of information. A broad, open-ended identification stage will counteract these problems. Consider availability, the bias of excessive focus on a single salient cue or item of information. An effective identification stage—in which the group looks at more than one solution and acquires information relevant to several options—is likely to reduce and eliminate availability effects, especially if there is some diversity within the group.

Framing effects are also a form of closed-minded thinking. If everyone in a group shares a single frame for the problem, it is likely that the group decision will amplify any biases produced by that perspective. Framing is one micromechanism underlying group polarization. An enhanced identification stage will increase the chances that an alternative view will be introduced into the discussion, thus reducing the tendency to polarize.

Confirmation bias can also be reduced by beginning with an open-ended group process; separating the two stages and enhancing the identification stage should improve performance further. Obviously, a rigorous identification process will reduce or eliminate egocentric biases, which are likely to remain at the group level only when there are traces of groupthink and overconformity in the first place. Hindsight bias can be viewed as a myopic focus on the outcome that actually occurred, making it difficult to regain the wide-open view of alternative possibilities that is characteristic of a realistic, future-directed view. Here too, open, unconstrained group discussion reduces the bias. An improved identification stage can help even more.

The planning fallacy is a form of myopia, focusing on one streamlined scenario. And again, a rigorous identification stage can shift the focus from one scenario to a more complex representation of the situation. At its best, rigorous identification techniques will simultaneously change the overall strategy from a so-called inside view to comparisons to relevant cases, or an outside view.[7]

Executing a separate and rigorous second selection stage can also reduce some judgment biases, especially those associated with incomplete thinking about the consequences and objectives of an action. Importantly, a thorough application of a future-oriented analysis will counteract the tendency to escalate a commitment to a losing strategy or to honor sunk costs.

We acknowledge that some biases are unlikely to be reduced by even an enhanced, two-stage process: these include those created by the representativeness heuristic, or similarity-based thinking. This powerful, intuitive habit is not simply a matter of myopic thinking and is not easily solvable with more-systematic evaluations. The only remedy that we know is training in analytic, statistical reasoning. With individual expertise and an organizational culture that promotes logical, data-based arguments, there is hope of counteracting the use of such heuristics.

Cost-Benefit Analysis

What, exactly, are more-systematic evaluations? We have suggested that they are based on more analytic thinking and on data. Within the federal government, systematic evaluation goes by a specific name: cost-benefit analysis. For regulatory decisions, President Reagan required such analysis in 1981. In particular, he said that to the extent permitted by law, regulatory agencies could not proceed with a regulation unless the benefits outweighed the costs and unless the chosen approach "maximized net benefits."

The latter requirement means that even if an agency identifies an approach with benefits in excess of costs, the agency has to investigate whether another approach might have even higher net benefits. Reagan's ideas applied across a spectacularly wide range, covering regulations meant to protect the environment, increase food safety, reduce risks on the highways and in the air, promote health care, improve immigration, affect the energy supply, or increase homeland security. Revealingly, Reagan's approach won bipartisan approval, and the requirements of cost-benefit balancing and of maximizing net benefits have been part of American government for well over thirty years.

A large part of Sunstein's job at OIRA was to promote compliance with those requirements. Within the federal government, cost-benefit balancing operates as an indispensable safeguard against behavioral biases. Suppose, for example, that bad incidents have occurred in the recent past—say, cases of food poisoning. There is a natural inclination to respond with a regulatory requirement. But would the requirement do much good? How much would it cost? Cost-benefit analysis puts a spotlight on the right questions.

When Sunstein was in government, a member of the president's cabinet once asked him, "Cass, how can you put a price on a human life?" That's a good question, but economists have an answer. (We'll spare you the details, but it's about $9 million. If that seems alarming, note that the better way to think about it is that if the government is eliminating a mortality risk of one in a hundred thousand, it would be willing to spend about $90. The reason is that evidence suggests that the average person would spend that amount to reduce a mortality risk of that magnitude.) Whether or not that answer is right, no government can or will spend an infinite amount to save a single life—which means that trade-offs are inevitable. We need to make the right ones.

Within government, cost-benefit analysis is an indispensable safeguard not only against individual biases, but also against group errors. If people are prone to availability bias, and thus too fearful (because a disaster has occurred in the recent past) or too complacent (because no such event has occurred), cost-benefit analysis imposes real discipline and helps to counteract the bias. And if group polarization leads people toward either extreme action or inaction, cost-benefit analysis imposes a reality check. Cost-benefit analysis also supplies numbers that weaken any particular framing effects. Time and again, cost-benefit analysis operates as a check both on individual error and on potentially large, even tragic mistakes at the group level. People are a lot safer, and the economy is a lot more efficient, as a result.

Often the best evidence informing the use of cost-benefit analysis comes from randomized controlled trials, by which researchers vary an aspect of a situation for one population and compare the outcomes to those for an otherwise similar population. In medicine, of course, randomized trials are the gold standard, telling us what treatments really work. Increasingly, policy analysts use such trials as well, asking (for example) whether a fee for the use of plastic bags really diminishes the use of such bags, or whether reductions in cell phone use have a beneficial effect on highway safety, or whether and to what extent people's eating habits change when they are informed of calorie counts. For businesses, randomized controlled trials are common as well, and they can provide a lot of information about products and innovations. We should expect far more use of such trials in the future—not least because they promise to overcome some of the problems associated with group decisions.

Although cost-benefit analysis is not our main topic here, it is important to emphasize that for the private and public sector, that form of analysis is increasingly feasible and is often the best safeguard at the selection stage. Big data, coming from randomized trials, can provide a lot of information about both costs and benefits—for example, about likely consumer reactions and about possible surprises. The best check on behavioral biases, at both the individual and the group level, is to get systematic about the facts. Moneyball works in baseball, and we have only started to see its potential in medicine, business, and government.

8

When Are
Crowds Wise?

We have noted that on many questions, the average or majority view of group members turns out to be stunningly accurate. One reason is that by polling all members and by avoiding social influences, groups make very efficient use of information. And if the groups are diverse and the judgments are independent, there is a lot of information to aggregate.

Imagine that a company is attempting to project its sales for certain products in the following year; maybe the company needs an accurate projection to know how much to spend on advertising and promotion. Might it do best to poll its salespeople and trust the average number?[1] Or suppose that a public official is deciding on whether to embark on a new program in the hope that the program would reduce unemployment. Should the official poll her advisers and take the average answer?

Many people, including most executives, would say, "No! Why settle for an *average* answer? We want the *best* answer." But this view, which is often based on the illusion of omniscience in hindsight, is wrong. The problem is that in foresight, before the judgment has been rendered, no one knows which individual has the best answer. In hindsight, it seems (too) easy. "We should have just relied on Fred; he had the answer." But of course, before the answer was known, no one knew for sure that Fred would be right. We return to this bad habit of chasing the expert in chapter 9.

The Condorcet Jury Theorem and the Law of Large Numbers

To understand why group averages and majority-rule judgments might be so accurate, we can learn much from a long historical tradition. A large part of the answer comes from the Condorcet Jury Theorem.[2] The Marquis de Condorcet, after whom the theorem is named, is one of the greatest social theorists of all time. Working in the eighteenth century, he used a little mathematics to produce some exceptionally important results. Condorcet was especially interested in how groups might aggregate the judgments of individuals. Writing around the time of the French Revolution, he was obsessed with the question of how to justify a shift from a dictatorial monarchy to a democracy. How could rule via the "voice of the people" be justified rationally?

To see how the Jury Theorem works, suppose that group members are all answering the same question, which has two possible answers, one false and one true. Assume too that the probability that each member will answer correctly exceeds 50 percent. The Jury Theorem says that the probability of a correct answer, by a majority of the group, increases toward 100 percent as the size of the group increases. This result holds if the members are only slightly more likely to be correct than incorrect, even far from 100 percent as individuals. The central point is that groups will do better than individuals, and big groups better than little ones, so long as two conditions are met: majority rule is used and each group member is more likely than not to be correct.

The theorem is not exactly intuitive, but it is based on some pretty simple arithmetic. Suppose, for example, that an employer has appointed a three-person team and that each member has a 67 percent probability of being right. The probability that a majority vote will choose the correct answer is 74 percent. As the size of the group increases, this probability increases too, at least so long as each member is more likely to be right than wrong. It should be clear that as the likelihood of a correct answer by individual members increases (say, from 60 percent to 70 percent), the likelihood of a correct answer by the group increases too, at least if majority rule is used. If group members are 80 percent likely to be right, and the group contains ten or more people, the probability of a correct answer by the majority is very close to 100 percent.

The importance of the Jury Theorem lies in its demonstration that so long as deliberation is not involved and the groups are purely statistical (in the sense that members are being polled independently, rather than influencing one another), they are likely to do better than individuals. Moreover, large groups are likely to do better than small ones, *if* majority rule is used and *if* each person is more likely than not to be correct. The point bears on decisions of all kinds of groups, including businesses, religious organizations, and of course political institutions.

The Condorcet Jury Theorem is essentially a more specific version of a very general statistical principle: the law of large numbers. The basic idea is that if the inputs have some kernel of truth to them (in the case of the Jury Theorem, the individuals are more likely to be right than wrong) *and* if they are relatively independent, then the more inputs, the more accurate the average or the majority answer. This was exactly the conclusion reached by Francis Galton about a century after Condorcet (we mentioned Galton's study in chapter 1). Interestingly, Galton was also motivated by the philosophical question of when "the crowd" will be wise (his paper was titled *Vox Populi*)—although Galton, who was something of an elitist, was surprised by the accuracy of the average estimate.[3] We have mentioned his study of fairgoers estimating the weight of a prize ox, where the average was within two pounds of the truth, and the median, the measure Galton favored for mathematical reasons, was within ten pounds; both crowd estimates beat the best individual estimator.

In addition to the benefit of many individual estimates, different perspectives or evidence also promote better answers or solutions. This kind of diversity is highly desirable and is almost certain to increase the quality of the solution selected or calculated.

In the case of estimating numerical answers, the value of diversity is easy to see. The key property of a sample of estimates of a single value is that the estimates are unbiased and equally likely to fall above or below the true value. If the individual estimates "bracket" the truth, then any degree of variability can be corrected when an average value is calculated, and the errors cancel one another out.[4]

To demonstrate the point, we have to use a little arithmetic.[5] Consider the number of nation states in the United Nations. Suppose two individuals estimate there are 250 and 150 (in 2014, the correct answer was 192). Those two estimates "bracket" the truth; 250 is 58 too high, while 150 is 42 too low. So their absolute errors (the difference between the individual's estimate and the actual number) are 58 and 42, and the average individual error is 50, or (58 + 42)/2.

But consider the average of the two estimates, or 200, with its much lower absolute error of only 8. If the estimates bracket the truth, the error of the *average estimate* will always be lower than the average error of the individual estimates. This means if individual estimates (two or more) bracket the truth, the average of the estimates will be more accurate than the individual estimates (which should be compared to the average of the individual errors).

Now what if the individual estimates do *not* bracket the truth and hence are all on the same side of the truth (either too high or too low)? In this situation, the error of the average estimate will always *equal* the average of the individual errors, but will not be worse. In the UN example, suppose the individual estimates were 200 and 250 (both too high and both on the same side of the truth). Then the individual errors would be 8 and 58, and the average of those individual errors would be 33. This is the same as the error of the average (the average is 225, and the error of that average is 225 − 192 = 33).

The conclusion is that the average estimate is always better (smaller error) if the individual estimates bracket the truth, and it is equal if all the individual estimates are over- or underestimates.

It follows that the average is always *at least as good* as a typical, representative individual. Bracketing is, of course, likelier when the estimates come from diverse sources that differ in background information, perspectives, or strategies to reach an answer. A more general version of this principle is the intuition that triangulation is a useful method to determine the validity of facts or procedures. If different lines of analysis or independent sources of evidence converge on a single answer, then that answer is more likely to be correct.[6]

But what if the group's estimators are not diverse? The answer is that the group average will still usually beat most individuals, but the advantage of averaging is reduced. The full power of error canceling, achieved when a truly diverse sample is obtained, with lots of bracketing of the truth, is lost. But although the average is biased, it is no more biased than the typical (also biased) individual.

The disadvantage of lack of diversity (that is, a dependency between the individual estimates) is compounded when the estimators communicate with one another or seek additional information. Then we see the polarization effect kicking in, and the individuals can be locked into a spiral of self-confirmatory discussions that make the group even more biased than it was when the individual estimates were not subjected to discussion.

Lots of Numbers

In the context of what we are calling statistical groups, several of Condorcet's stringent assumptions are met. Indeed, the likelihood that they will be met is higher with statistical groups than with deliberating ones. Condorcet assumed that (1) people would be unaffected by whether their votes would be decisive, (2) people would be unaffected by one another's votes, and (3) the probability that one group member would be correct would be statistically unrelated to the probability that another group member would be correct.[7]

The first two assumptions plainly hold for statistical groups, such as those assessing the number of beans in a jar, the weight of prize livestock, or the number of purchases of a new product. People do not know what others are saying, and hence they cannot be influenced by social pressure to conform with other members of the group. The third assumption may or may not be violated. Those who have similar training or who work closely together will be likely to see things in the same way, possibly leading to a violation of the third assumption. On the other hand, the Condorcet Jury Theorem has been shown to work even in the face of violations of this third assumption; we put the technical complexities to the side here.[8]

To get a clearer sense of why statistical groups often perform so well, note that even if everyone in the group is not more than 50 percent likely to be right, the theorem's optimistic predictions may well continue to hold. Suppose, for example, that 60 percent of people are 51 percent likely to be right and that 40 percent of people are 50 percent likely to be right; or that 45 percent of people are 40 percent likely to be right and that 55 percent of people are 65 percent likely to be right; or even that 51 percent of people are 51 percent likely to be right and that 49 percent of people are merely 50 percent likely to be right. Even under these conditions, the likelihood of a correct answer, via majority vote, will move toward 100 percent as the size of the group increases. It will not move as quickly as it would if every group member were highly likely to be right, but it will nonetheless move.

We could imagine endless variations on these particular numbers. Even if some or many group members are more likely to be wrong than right, a majority vote can produce the correct answer if many other members are more likely to be right and if the group is big enough. Consider another possibility, one with great practical importance: 40 percent of group members are more likely than not to be right, and 60 percent are only 50 percent likely to be right, but the errors of the 60 percent are *entirely random*. Because those who blunder do so randomly, the group, if it is big enough, will still end up with the right answer.

Here is the reason, which follows from our account of the law of large numbers: if a core of people have some insight into what's right, and if the rest of the group make genuinely random errors, the majority will be driven in the direction set by the core. Suppose that a thousand people are asked the name of the actor who played Katniss in the *Hunger Games* movies. If 40 percent of the group choose Jennifer Lawrence (the right answer, of course), and if the other 60 percent make random guesses, Jennifer Lawrence will emerge with the highest number of votes.

Lots of Possibilities

In studies of statistical groups, most judgments do not involve a binary choice, that is, a choice between just two possibilities. The easiest cases for use of the Jury Theorem ask a simple yes-or-no question. Compare the very different question of how many beans are in a jar, how many pounds a given object weighs, how many bombs a nation has, how many copies of a certain book will sell, and how much money an investment will make in the following year. When many options are offered, will the Jury Theorem hold?

Note first that in answering such questions, each person is effectively being asked to answer a long series of binary questions—ten beans or a thousand, twenty beans or five hundred, fifty beans or one hundred, and so on. If a big-enough group is asked to answer such questions, and if most individual answers are better than chance, the average answer is likely to be highly accurate.

Unfortunately, the combination of probabilities for a series of binary results might mean that things will turn out poorly. If someone is 51 percent likely to answer each of two questions correctly, the probability that he will answer *both* questions correctly is only slightly higher than 25 percent. Suppose that you are 51 percent likely to be right on whether there are 800 or 780 beans in a jar and 51 percent likely to be right on whether there are 780 or 760 beans in a jar. Sad to say, you're almost 75 percent likely to get either one or both of the two questions wrong, and things get rapidly worse as the number of questions increases.

If someone is 51 percent likely to answer each of five questions correctly, the likelihood that he will answer all five questions correctly is very small—a little over 3 percent. But with many large groups, the average answer will nonetheless be quite accurate. Here is the key point, again a product of the law of large numbers: if a significant number of people are more likely to choose the correct question than any of the incorrect ones, and if errors are randomly distributed, then the average judgment will be quite reliable.

More-technical analysis offers a nice result for people who are interested in using statistical groups, which is that even with a range of options, the correct outcome is more likely to attract plurality support than any of the others.[9] The central idea is that if group members face three or more choices, the likelihood that the best option will win a plurality increases with the size of the group *if* each individual member is more likely to vote for the best option than for any of the others. As the number of members expands to infinity, the likelihood that the correct answer will be the plurality's choice increases to 100 percent.

The mathematical details are not important. What matters is that there is good reason to think that employers and others might reasonably conclude that it makes sense to ask a lot of people and to rely on the average or majority answer.

The Dark Side of the Jury Theorem

Unfortunately, the Jury Theorem has a dark side, which also has important implications. Most important, there is a variation on a problem we have already encountered: "garbage in, garbage out." Suppose that most people in a group are more likely to be wrong than right, maybe because they suffer from some kind of behavioral bias. If so, the likelihood that the group's majority will decide correctly falls to *zero* as the size of the group increases!

Here is an important warning: groups should not be carried away by the seductive illusion of accuracy of statistical averages in every circumstance. Accuracy can be found only under certain conditions—most importantly, those in which many or most people are likely to be right. If group members are inclined in the wrong direction, it would be a mistake to rely on statistical averages.

To see the problem more concretely, imagine that a group consists of a number of people, each of whom is at least 51 percent likely to be mistaken. The group might be a small business, a political party, a religious organization, or a law firm. The probability that the group will err approaches 100 percent as its size expands. Condorcet himself explicitly signaled this possibility and its source: "In effect, when the probability of the truth of a voter's opinion falls below ½, there must be a reason why he decides less well than one would at random. The reason can only be found in the prejudices to which this voter is subject."[10]

If group members are prejudiced in some way, the average answer is likely to be way off. Moreover, the errors might stem not only from literal prejudices, but also from confusion, ignorance, poor information-processing, or simple incompetence. On hard questions requiring specialized knowledge, there is no reason to think that the average answer of group members will be right. So too on complex issues involving business or politics. And even if people are competent, they might well be led astray, especially if they are dealing with highly technical questions.

We have emphasized that individuals are subject to a wide range of biases uncovered by behavioral scientists. As noted earlier, the optimistic bias means that most people show a systematic tendency toward unrealistic optimism.[11] There is good reason to think that in both business and politics, optimistic bias is a pervasive problem. If group members are unrealistically optimistic, then statistical groups will reflect that bias, producing mistaken judgments. If a company's senior managers think that a product is bound to succeed and if they are unrealistically optimistic, the group is not well served by relying on the view of the average member. And if those involved in a political campaign think that their candidate is best and that voters will inevitably concur with this opinion, the systematic bias will be reflected in the average view within the group. (Recall that in 2012, many supporters of Mitt Romney believed that Romney would win, even though all the empirical evidence suggested otherwise.)

Of course, falsehoods are often the conventional wisdom. And in many contexts, group members are in fact likely to blunder. Joseph Henrich and his coauthors offer some examples of misguided beliefs: "Many Germans believe that drinking water after eating cherries is deadly; they also believe that putting ice in soft drinks is unhealthy. The English, however, rather enjoy a cold drink of water after some cherries; and Americans love icy refreshments."[12] At least one group must be wrong. If most people in certain countries believe that the United States was itself responsible for the terrorist attacks in New York on 9/11—and they do—then large groups have badly blundered. In short, the optimistic conclusion of the Jury Theorem holds only if we assume a certain level of accuracy on the part of the people involved. That assumption might be heroic.

Biases and Blunders

With the dark side of the Jury Theorem in mind, we should see that a systematic bias in one or another direction will create problems for the answers of statistical groups. Suppose that Arab terrorists were asked about the recent history of the United States, or that men with misogynist attitudes were asked to evaluate women's abilities. Major errors would be inevitable, however large the number of people involved. Or suppose that some bias is leading group members to favor one or another product (say, a new tablet or automobile) or even a candidate for public office; perhaps most of the members have been manipulated or misled. The dark side of the Jury Theorem ensures that big mistakes will result from relying on averages. Condorcet was fully alert to this problem, saying that it is "necessary, furthermore, that voters be enlightened; and that they be the more enlightened, the more complicated the question upon which they decide."[13]

If they rely on statistical averages, legislatures and executive officers may make bad decisions for this very reason. Speaking of democracy in general, Condorcet made the point clearly, calling it "a rather important observation": "A very numerous assembly cannot be composed of very enlightened men. It is even probable that those comprising this assembly will on many matters combine great ignorance with many prejudices. Thus there will be a great number of questions on which the probability of the truth of each voter will be below ½. It follows that the more numerous the assembly, the more it will be exposed to the risk of making false decisions."[14]

Condorcet contended that because of the risk of pervasive prejudice and ignorance, "it is clear that it can be dangerous to give a democratic constitution to an unenlightened people." And even in societies with relatively enlightened people, he believed that citizens should not make decisions themselves, but should generally be restricted to the role of electing representatives, "those whose opinions will have a large enough probability of being true."[15] Condorcet was speaking of very large groups, but his observation also holds for small ones whenever the average view may be wrong.

The Payoff: When Should Groups Use Averages?

For groups, it would be a big mistake to suggest that the best approach to hard questions is *always* to ask a large number of people and to take the average answer. That approach is likely to work only under particular circumstances: those in which many or most people are more likely than not to be right. Such circumstances might be found when, for example, a company president is asking a group of informed advisers about the proper course of action, or when a dean at a university is asking the faculty whether to hire a certain job candidate, or when a head of a government agency is consulting a group of scientists about whether a particular pollution problem is likely to be serious. In all of these cases, there might well be reason to trust the people who are being asked, and if so, the average answer is likely to be right.

The law of large numbers has another implication. If you know little about the truth, cannot correctly select the most accurate individual judges beforehand, and suspect systematic biases in the individual estimates, then you should still go with the average estimate. In the absence of better information (including knowledge of the direction of the individuals' biases), it is better to rely on the average. An average will be biased, but still more accurate than a typical individual member. And again, diversity is your friend.

The implications for group behavior are mixed. To the extent that the goal is to arrive at the correct judgments on facts, the Condorcet Jury Theorem affords no guarantees. In numerous domains, too many people are likely to blunder in systematic ways. Wise groups fully recognize this point. Now let's turn to the question of expertise and how groups might best harness it—a question that has a close connection to the Jury Theorem.

9

How to Harness Experts

Many managers are inclined to rely on experts. Before we evaluate that practice, we need to say a few words about expertise. It's obvious that the term can be understood in many ways. Here we mean expertise in the sense of *being able to make winning bets on the future.* This ability could be shown implicitly through the capacity to come up with a good design—as, for example, by building a bridge or another structure that performs well in an uncertain future of storms and erosion, or by designing an investment strategy that really is risk-proof. More relevant to our concerns here is the ability to make accurate forecasts about uncertain future events.

Unfortunately, very few so-called experts can make good predictions. When most experts are put to a careful test, they prove to be much less competent than popular opinion expects (or than they themselves claim). In most professions, telling a pleasing and convincing story, rather than making accurate predictions, is the primary evidence relied on to assign someone the label *expert*. Often those stories are told after the fact, not in advance, and when they are told in advance, they tend to have more superficial plausibility than factual accuracy.

Political pundits who have been "scored" on the accuracy of their election forecasts are generally found to perform at chance or even worse.[1] Similar conclusions apply to popular stock-pickers, many of whom turn out to be a bit like astrologers. A pathbreaking book by the social scientist Philip Tetlock finds that for a wide range of events, professional experts turn out to be pretty terrible forecasters.[2] And in fact, the book provides data showing that the popularity and public visibility of an expert is negatively correlated with his or her accuracy. Sadly, it seems for pundits, confidence trumps accuracy.

To be sure, there are some clear cases of documented expertise, including weather forecasters, physicists (forecasting sunspots and other astronomical phenomena), chess and bridge experts, and some professionals in branches of medicine and financial auditing.[3] The key to knowing when experts can make accurate predictions is to understand two factors: the conditions surrounding their training and the environment in which they make their forecasts.

One form of expertise derives from a sound scientific understanding of the particular domain in which judgments are made. In physics, meteorology, engineering, and some areas of medicine and finance, there are empirically validated theoretical frameworks and well-established forecasting and diagnostic methods. The same is true in sports, especially baseball, where experts, armed with statistical methods, can make pretty good predictions about player performance (as celebrated and made famous by *Moneyball*). When experts are trained in the relevant theories and methods, perhaps assisted by analytic software programs, it is reassuring that they can turn the vast foundation of scientific wisdom into accurate predictions.

Nate Silver's distinctive ability to predict political election outcomes is an example of this form of expertise.[4] Rather than responding on the basis of his intuition, experiences, or prejudices about who should win an election, Silver relies on hundreds of years of statistical theory and practice, interpreting the results of polls to make forecasts. Silver's very public success has led to a small (and entirely justified) burst of indignation about the lousy track records of many other publicly identified political experts.[5]

A second form of expertise is experiential, not theory based, and is derived from training, often via apprenticeships in which the learner gets quick and precise feedback while making many practice judgments. This kind of expertise takes the form of "knowing what to look for" and is often summarized in advice about how to make assessments.[6]

For example, most livestock judges are extremely accurate when asked to estimate the market value or breeding quality of a prize ox or sow. They learn this skill through an extensive apprenticeship in which they make thousands of such judgments, are required to defend each judgment, and then receive immediate feedback from more-senior experts. A similar training regimen applies to certified weather forecasters, who are also assisted by expert software and long study of meteorological theory. In these cases, careful behavioral analysis has found that the judge's expertise is best described as knowing which particular aspects of the situation to study and then how to combine the information from those cues into a judgment.

The third form of expertise is also based on experience with many thousands of example cases, again followed by quick, precise feedback. This form of expertise was first identified as underlying the remarkable skills of chess players by the Nobel Prize–winning behavioral scientist Herbert Simon and his colleague Bill Chase.[7] These scientists were intrigued by the question of chess expertise (what separates the world–class players from the novices) and especially by the puzzle of why grandmasters' skill hardly declined in speed-chess matches, where moves are made in seconds, not minutes.

Their conclusion was that the thousands of hours studying past games led to the development of an elaborate expert memory store of tens of thousands of mental snapshots of chessboard configurations with stored best-move "answers" for each snapshot. Many other examples of this form of expert capacity have been identified in subsequent research in fields ranging from sports skills to medical wisdom.[8] In addition to the athletic ability to execute offensive strategies, a great football quarterback has a mental library of visual images that instantly identify configurations of defenders to support that uncanny ability to read the defense and select targets for pass reception. Champion tennis players have the same kind of mental library. A similar snapshot-matching process underlies the diagnostic skills of experienced dermatologists and radiologists.[9]

These three thinking skills—theory-based reasoning, knowledge about which valid cues to use, and case-based memory-matching—are the primary forms of expertise identified by behavioral scientists. We know of no other credible forms of verified judgmental expertise.

There are two important points to remember. First, a reliable capacity to predict the future with better-than-modest accuracy is very rare. Second, some highly specific forms of expertise do exist. So, if you are attempting to leverage intelligence out of a collective, be sure you start with a sample of *verified* experts.

If you start with such experts, you might well end up doing a lot better than if you take a general sample of the population and rely on its average answer. Real experts will almost certainly do better than statistical averages of amateurs. Even here, however, there are some important lessons for wise groups to keep in mind.

Enlisting Expertise

We should now understand that performance depends on the competence of the individuals making the relevant judgments. Suppose that we could find real experts in estimating the weight of oxen or in counting jelly beans; suppose too that we understand expertise to be the ability to make accurate assessments. If so, then these (admittedly weird and obsessive) experts would, by definition, do better than statistical averages. In the real world, we must often choose between a small group of people, each with a large amount of information, and a large group of people, each with a small amount of information. Everything depends on the levels of expertise; sometimes the large group is worse.

One thing is clear: whether we are dealing with experts or non-experts, it makes sense to obtain a statistical answer from a group of them, rather than to depend on one or a few. If experts are likely to be right, a statistical group of experts should have exactly the same advantage over individual experts as a statistical group of ordinary people has over ordinary individuals. Many expert minds are likely to be better than a few.

A great deal of evidence supports this claim.[10] In a series of thirty comparisons, statistical groups of experts had 12.5 percent fewer errors than individual experts on forecasting tasks involving such diverse issues as cattle and chicken prices, real and nominal gross national product, survival of patients, and housing starts.[11] So too, statistical groups of experts significantly outperformed individual experts in predicting the annual earnings of firms, changes in the American economy, and annual peak rainfall runoff.[12] For groups, the implication is straightforward. In forecasting expert Scott Armstrong's words, "organizations often call on the best expert they can find to make important forecasts. They should avoid this practice, and instead combine forecasts from a number of experts."[13] Leaders of companies and nations, please take note.

For political polling, it has become standard practice to combine several poll results and, just as with individual human forecasters, to rely on the average or median, rather than to select one or two. This practice has had excellent results. There is a general lesson here for predictions about electoral outcomes. When forecasters lack enough different polls on the same question, they should instead use multiple indicators—a range of diverse questions that tap into the same underlying factor. The answer might be averaged into some kind of composite, one that is likely to be more reliable than individual items.

No Chasing

These points bear on the decisions of businesses and governments alike. The problem is that people, including leaders, are usually unwilling to use averages of experts. Instead, the norm is to chase the expert, in an effort, usually futile, to beat the average by identifying the single most accurate thinker. This unfortunate habit might well be a by-product of the ubiquitous hindsight bias. After the fact, we know exactly who was closest to the truth, and this knowledge makes us forget that we had no clue about who was the most accurate before the fact.

Chasing the expert is usually a terrible idea, as a study by Albert Mannes and his colleagues demonstrated.[14] They asked Duke University MBAs to play the financial forecasting game staged twice a year by the *Wall Street Journal*. The public contest pitted economic experts against one another in forecasting salient economic trends such as interest rates and unemployment statistics. The MBAs were asked to make forecasts for twenty-four periods. They were able to rely on either the best single expert (according to past predictions) or an average of the predictions of all the experts.

The results were dramatic: 80 percent of the MBAs picked the single best expert. How did chasing the expert serve them? Not well. Under all experimental conditions, chasing the expert performed significantly worse than relying on the average of all experts.

Still, if we decide to consult all the experts, is there a better way to combine their judgments than a simple average? Here we get to the frontiers of behavioral science wisdom. A helpful source is a large-scale research project funded by the Office of the Director of National Intelligence.[15] Several teams of researchers addressed the question of how to improve intelligence analysis in forecasts of political, diplomatic, and economic events. The emerging conclusion is that there is some improvement if we weight individual experts by their track record of prior forecasts for similar events. So the Duke MBAs were right to think the best expert was the most informative, but they overreacted and ignored the information contained in other experts' estimates.

A collateral finding from the intelligence-forecasting tournament was that the experts' self-evaluations of their own judgments were not useful. Weighting the experts' judgments by each expert's own self-confidence did not improve accuracy of the composite; experts lacked subjective insights into their own performance. Only weighting by objective "batting averages" of measured past accuracy was helpful.

The lesson is clear: do not be misled by expert bravado or by an expert's own sense of how he or she is doing. Evidence is a much better guide than an impressive self-presentation.

10

Tips for Using Tournaments

For a very long time, managers have used tournaments and other contests, whether formal or informal, to encourage good ideas and to spark creativity. But with respect to tournaments, we're entering a whole new age. Let's take a look at a highly publicized example, the Netflix Prize contest, and then try to extract some more general lessons.

The Netflix Prize

Netflix, one of the major providers of rental and video-on-demand entertainment content, is an innovative and trend-setting company. It does a lot of its own research and development.

A distinctive feature of its website—a feature that draws many customers to the business—is its movie recommendation service, Cinematch. If you like *House of Cards*, you'll probably like *Mad Men*, and if you like *Star Trek*, you'll probably like *Twilight Zone*, and if you like *Air Bud Spikes Back*, you'll probably like *Super Buddies* (don't ask).

The concept of Cinematch originated at Bell Labs, which is also renowned for its innovative capabilities, including the invention of the electronic transistor. Bell's scientists were trying to improve the services of web-based Yellow Pages. They hit on the idea of recommending services to inquirers, on the basis of the successful past recommendations to *similar* customers. Through Bell's user database, a new customer would be matched with other customers who had entered similar queries or had provided similar satisfaction ratings on services obtained through the automated Yellow Pages.

For example, a female, middle-aged, Caucasian, Protestant accountant might be matched to several other similar users and then provided with "answers" to her queries; the answers were slanted to include recommendations that had pleased the similar users. Netflix applied the same case-based similarity algorithms in its Cinematch feature to recommend movies to its customers. And with a few amusing exceptions, customers were happy and often surprised by the usefulness of the Cinematch recommendations.

In 2006, Netflix decided to make a substantial upgrade in the quality of its recommendations. But instead of simply sending the problem to its own in-house engineers, Netflix advertised a $1 million prize for the first algorithm to beat Cinematch by 10 percent (a reduction in the rate of errors in the recommendations). The contest's rules were carefully spelled out. For example, the criteria for a winning submission were defined precisely; the conditions of the test to verify those criteria were specified; and "training data" were provided publicly to all competitors so that they could fine-tune and test their algorithms before submitting them to Netflix. It took only four days for a competitor to beat Cinematch's performance, but a 10 percent reduction in error is substantial, and the contest ran for three years before a winner was declared. (Perhaps not coincidentally, it was a team from Bell Labs.)

What is most amazing, at least to us, is the extraordinary investment of effort that was produced by the $1 million incentive. Over twenty thousand teams from more than 150 nations joined the competition. In the endgame, more than ten teams of elite engineers were putting more time into the competition than into their day jobs. Compare this result with the much more modest effort that would have been produced with a $1 million investment in in-house R&D.

Overcoming Failures of Deliberation

Notice also how the innovation tournament (as an economist would call it) solves the problems faced by deliberating groups. First, the dispersion of teams across the globe—connected to the contest only through the internet—meant that there was independence. Second, the teams did not share methods (only performance results). And finally, the winner-take-all character of the tournament (only one team can win) incentivizes divergent strategies, including attempts to hit the jackpot with a completely novel strategy.

This cocktail of conditions and incentives, promoting independent and deliberately divergent thinking, prevents a misstep or blind alley from being propagated and amplified across teams. Cascades will not occur if no one knows where the others are headed and, furthermore, if everyone is motivated to run in unique directions in the first place. And although individual teams may pursue extreme solutions, the competitors as a whole are unlikely to become polarized in a single direction.

Netflix's precision in the statement of the task conditions and the objectives (criteria for winning) ensured that most teams stayed focused on the problem of interest. Fuzzy contest rules (e.g., the traditional in-house suggestion-box contest) are unlikely to yield the kind of focused but widespread and energetic participation produced by the Netflix Prize.

InnoCentive and Beyond

As we have noted, innovation tournaments have been around for centuries, but with the rise of the internet, their scale and frequency have jumped up dramatically. One of the famous historical examples was the Longitude Prize of £20,000 offered by the British government in 1714 for a method that would determine a ship's longitudinal location precisely (within thirty nautical miles). The large prize was never paid out, but many small prizes were awarded for advances that contributed to improved nautical location. Now numerous companies are creating innovation tournaments through their own sites or implementing them in-house if they do not want to publicize their own R&D strategies.

Consider just a few examples. In 2013, General Electric publicly posted the GE Engine Bracket Challenge, with a $20,000 prize, and the company received almost seven hundred solutions for an engineering problem involving lighter mounting brackets for an aircraft engine.[1] Eight solutions were close enough to split the prize, and GE integrated the complementary parts of those solutions to create a new bracket that is 80 percent lighter than the prior solution.

In the same year, the Pentagon paid a $2 million prize to a Stanford University team whose robotic car won a 132-mile race. Also in 2013, the Breakthrough Prize in Life Sciences announced that it would pay $3 million in awards for medically relevant innovations. A new start-up (BattleFin) uses contests with prizes in the thousands of dollars to identify mathematical talent for commercial financial analysis.

In this context, the best-known practitioner is InnoCentive, a technically oriented firm that matches "seekers" with more than three hundred thousand registered "solvers," over half from Asia and Eastern Europe, through bulletin board postings. Essentially, InnoCentive serves as a referee guaranteeing that only well-formed problems are posted. The company verifies solutions and oversees award payments, usually in the range of $10,000 to $100,000. InnoCentive will also deal with the legal contracts that give the intellectual-property rights for solutions to the solvers, after solutions have been found.

We have mentioned the extraordinary capacity of well-designed innovation tournaments to evoke and maintain high levels of performance. For cases like the Netflix Prize, there are undoubtedly novelty effects, and of course, there are reputational incentives that probably overshadow the $1 million prize money. A huge professional audience of computer scientists remembers that BellKor's Pragmatic Chaos team (from Bell Labs) won the Netflix Prize, and in that world, the winning team's members are celebrities.

But even without those bonuses, the tournaments conducted through InnoCentive and other companies produce large investments of ingenuity and hard work by world-class engineers and scientists. There's a lesson here for businesses, both large and small, which can experiment with tournaments of their own. Even modest rewards can have big dividends, especially because of the reputational benefits that accompany a victory.

Why Tournaments Work

It is no coincidence that tournaments are the most effective market mechanism known in economics to promote elite performance at the top of the competitors' capacities. This is why we see tournaments everywhere in sports; they are also frequently used to distribute top-end bonuses to software engineers, sales personnel, and so forth. Furthermore, sharply declining payoff schedules (winner-take-all is the extreme on this continuum), like the prizes in professional golf or tennis, motivate the most elite of the elite to extraordinary achievements.

Other helpful features of the InnoCentive method include the anonymity of the competitors (no one knows the exact skill levels of their competitors), the prospect of developing a personal reputation or a long-term relationship with the "solver" (e.g., a job offer), and the role of the internet as a gateway to significantly better financial rewards than those available in local economies in China, India, and East Europe.

What is not so clear is how tournament methods affect information sharing. As with prediction markets, there are no clear incentives for sharing information with other parties. In fact, competitive organizations and institutions tend to discourage information sharing. It's obvious that private information is power, and the route to the ultimate payoff in a tournament, or a competitive investment institution like a pari-mutuel betting market, is keeping the good information secret. If you're trying to win the Netflix Prize, you don't want to share your ideas with competitors (you'll reduce your own chances of winning). If you're betting at the racetrack, you don't want to share valid tips with other bettors (you'll reduce the value of your own bets in a system where winners split the betting pool).

Despite the incentive not to share information in a competitive setting, one behavioral curiosity did occur toward the end of the Netflix challenge: to our surprise (and that of other behavioral scientists we've talked to), several teams that were close to winning combined their efforts in a final sprint to the finish line. We don't fully understand why the teams did this, but there might have been some reason to believe that continuing alone would not win the prize, and that a close collaboration would achieve the ultimate goal. But even without information sharing, tournaments can be a great idea, because they produce the right incentives to motivate high levels of investment by elite performers.

Designing an Effective Tournament: Numbers? Prizes?

The discussion thus far suggests three practical lessons about how to set up an effective problem-solving or decision-making tournament. First, make sure there is a well-defined rule to determine the winner. Second, provide a trustworthy umpire to decide the winner. Third, advertise the tournament widely to an audience of potential competitors who have the expertise and tools to create viable solutions. In a nutshell, it is good practice to define the problem clearly enough so that solvers who have a chance to win can self-select into the competition.

But two questions remain open: How many competitors should be encouraged to participate in a tournament? And how should prizes be structured? In other words, is a winner-take-all, single prize the most effective incentive to produce good solutions?

How Many Should Play?

With respect to the question of how many competitors to encourage, keep in mind the fact that the more competitors there are, the less likely any one competitor is to win. Increased numbers can therefore discourage the effort expended by every competitor. In the case of problems with well-defined solutions, only those who have a chance to solve those problems will enter, ensuring that there will be a vigorous contest among serious contenders.

The difficulty is that as uncertainty about who might win the prize increases (as is likely to be the case in many of the problems that companies and governments have been placing in tournaments), the increased size of the competition will demotivate all individual competitors. This conclusion follows directly not only from economic theory but also from common sense, because competitors will consider the costs and benefits of their actions in deciding what to do. As the chance of victory is reduced, the benefits of investing in the competition decrease.

At the same time, there is a psychological wrinkle. As we have seen, human beings tend to be unrealistically optimistic, and if competitors have that characteristic, then they might give it a shot even when they ought not to do so. To our knowledge, only one study has tested this question empirically, and it suggests that large numbers of competitors can indeed reduce effort.

In 2011, Kevin Boudreau and his colleagues analyzed the results of several hundred TopCoder contests to see if the number of competitors was related to individual effort.[2] TopCoder is a repeated competition to solve a wide variety of software coding problems. Competitors sign up for a competition by problem type (e.g., algorithms), and at a designated start time, they receive a problem and have seventy-five minutes to come up with a solution. An example problem might be: "Find the most popular person in a social network of differing ethnicities in the least amount of computation time."

Hundreds of thousands of programmers from all over the world participate to win professional acclaim and to establish an overall performance score across contests that can lead to better jobs as well as cash prizes. The key feature of TopCoder contests, which supports a behavioral analysis of a number of competitors, is that the contests are segregated into virtual rooms, with up to twenty players per room, and a first prize and other prizes are awarded to each room. (And of course, it's important that there is a reliable refereed score for each player.)

The authors' analysis confirmed that the more participants, the lower the competitors' effort. This was true at every level of performance. Even the top fifth of competitors, who had a realistic shot at winning, slowed down on the coding task if there were many competitors.

However, other researchers have suggested that the situation is more complicated—that increasing the numbers of players has other effects besides discouraging effort. A few years before

Boudreau and his colleagues' study, Christian Terwiesch and Yi Xu conjectured that more players meant less effort per player, but also, especially with more complex problems, that more players increased the chance of finding a truly novel solution (even with lower effort per player).[3] Terwiesch and Xu call this second factor the "parallel-paths" effect, referring to the observation that more competitors means that a greater number of different but parallel paths will be explored by competitors searching for a solution. That's good news.

Boudreau and his colleagues also found empirical evidence for the parallel-paths effect. Although most players put less effort into the task, the absolute best solution was usually better with more players. Other theorists have speculated that with more competitors in an enterprise (e.g., a tournament), the players are likelier to try truly novel paths to the solution—the parallel-paths effect.[4] On top of these results, Boudreau and his colleagues concluded that the more difficult a problem, the greater the positive parallel-paths effect and the smaller the discouragement effect.

In light of these opposing forces and the complexity of innovative endeavors, it is premature to give precise advice to a manager who wants to use a tournament to solve a problem or make a decision. Furthermore, the only empirical basis we have for such advice is the excellent study by Boudreau and colleagues, but theirs is not a study of innovation tournaments; it's a study of a contest with well-defined, known best answers.

Our best advice is to restrict participation to fewer competitors if the problem is routine—meaning that everyone agrees that a solution is close at hand. But for truly challenging problems, the kinds of problems that may not be solvable with present methods, open the competition up widely. This advice is somewhat different from the claim that it is always best to seek the highest participation levels possible—a claim sometimes made in work on crowdsourcing innovation.[5]

In the design of a tournament, the most important task is the careful specification of the objectives that must be optimized by the winning solution. The more precise the objectives, the more likely that the people best able to achieve remarkable solutions will be drawn to participate. Clarity about the criteria for winning may be even more important than the number of competitors or the prize payoff structure.

Deciding on the Nature of the Prize

What is the best policy for assigning prizes for solutions? In most current innovation tournaments, the rule is that only one competitor can win—winner takes all. But this rule does not accord with practices in analogous tournaments in, for example, professional sports, where there is prize money for several top performers (although the amounts drop off sharply from the first-place payoff).

Economic theories of incentives in tournaments usually prescribe multiple payoffs, with the exact distribution contingent on players' skill levels and risk attitudes. In innovation tournaments, which are not as numerous as sports tournaments (or TopCoder contests), considerable motivation can be produced by ancillary benefits, like reputation in the professional community, promotions within a company, and other payoffs from career signaling. We think that offering a few prizes, and not just one, is the way to go. The offer of more than a single prize tends to increase incentives by broadening the class of winners, without losing anything significant. So make it a winner-takes-a-lot contest; but we recommend against winner-takes-all.

Government by Tournament

In recent years, the US government has noticed the extraordinary potential of tournaments and prizes, and it has taken a number of steps to promote them. Let's take a look at the enthusiastic words of the government itself:

> For example, Defense Advanced Research Projects Agency's "grand challenges" have advanced the state of the art of robotic cars that drive themselves. The National Aeronautics and Space Administration's (NASA) Centennial Challenges have triggered an outpouring of creative solutions from students, citizen inventors, and entrepreneurial firms for technologies such as lunar landers, space elevators, fuel-efficient aircraft, and astronaut gloves. The Department of Energy has sponsored the L Prize, designed to spur the development of high-quality, highly efficient solid-state lighting products to replace today's inefficient light bulbs. The Environmental Protection Agency has used prizes to encourage students and others to develop videos to promote environmental stewardship. The Department of State has sponsored highly successful video and writing contests that have attracted contestants from a broad diversity of countries and geographic regions, and that have furthered the U.S. public diplomacy mission.[6]

Formal guidance from the Obama administration shows a lot of enthusiasm for the use of tournaments and offers a series of requirements designed to ensure that agencies use tournaments and that they are consistent with law.[7] The many successes to date suggest that there is a great deal of potential for groups within government to enlist tournaments to produce innovative solutions.

In September 2010, the Obama administration launched Challenge.gov, an online listing of incentive prizes offered by federal government agencies.[8] Four months later, President Obama signed into law the America COMPETES Reauthorization Act, which provides clear legal authority for all agencies to hold prize competitions to spur innovation.[9] Within its first two years, the site listed challenges from forty-five agencies and engaged more than sixteen thousand participants.[10] The challenges spanned the breadth of government programs, including a $10,000 State Department prize for new ideas for implementing arms control and nonproliferation treaties and a $160,000 prize from the EPA and the Department of Health and Human Services for portable systems to monitor and report on local air quality.[11]

The Challenge.gov program and America COMPETES Reauthorization Act have led to a number of evident success stories, including the creation of a consumer-friendly web portal for the National Cancer Institute—a portal that provides prospective patients with information about clinical trials for cancer and other diseases.[12] The Air Force Research Lab used the results of a competition to create a prototype system for air-dropping large humanitarian-aid packages of food and water into populated areas without damaging the packages or injuring bystanders.[13]

For our purposes, the most informative example of an innovation tournament within government was conducted by the Office of the Director of Intelligence through the Intelligence Advanced Research Projects Agency (IARPA). The tournament was called the Aggregative Contingent Estimation Program (or IARPA-ACE). The overarching objective was to invent methods to improve intelligence analysis and forecasts in a verifiable manner. As with the Netflix Prize, specific ground rules, one precise metric for assessing success, and some benchmark performance standards were provided to define the contest.

Five university-industry teams were selected, and each team was given approximately $1 million for the first year of the contest. A sixth organization—the "umpires"—was paid to supervise the tournament, to design a level playing field of about one hundred individual forecasting problems per year, and to track the overall performance scores of the research teams. All such teams were required to score their performance on a single metric—the same one used to evaluate weather forecasters. And once a year, each team had to submit one best procedure to the umpires, who would test all five methods with a sample of new forecasters on one set of identical test questions.

In this tournament, the ultimate prizes were the continued funding and professional acclaim from discovering high-performing methods. These kinds of incentives for the competitors have the advantage of allowing the sponsors, from IARPA, to require the teams to share their best results in a timely manner. Annual meetings and written progress reports were shared by all the competitors so that the teams could profit by learning from all the other teams as well as their own. Full disclosure of each team's discoveries was guaranteed, because these reports determined whether IARPA continued to allocate funding to participate in the tournament.

Methods of this kind will generally be useful for solving many business and government estimation and strategy problems, as the individual forecasting problems were representative of the kinds of forecasts made in many domains of human activity. The questions included these: Will Bashar al-Assad still be the president of Syria six months from today? Will Greece leave the European Union sometime before the end of this calendar year? Will a North

Korean military force fire on, or invade, South Korea in the next six months? Will Vladimir Putin be reelected as president of Russia?

Different research teams tended to specialize in distinct approaches to improving these forecasts. One group focused on statistical weighting and other mathematical adjustments to integrate individual estimates; one focused on prediction markets (see chapter 11); one focused on the Delphi method (see chapter 6); one on forecasters who communicated socially via chat rooms; and one on leveraging the independence and diversity of the individual estimates.

A lot has been discovered, so far, by the teams competing in this tournament. Averaging is good, as per our comments on the wisdom of crowds. Averaging by weighting individual estimates by the *objective* past records for accuracy on similar judgments is better; and additional improvements can be obtained by averaging updated beliefs with prior estimates (and weighting the most recent estimates more than those in the distant past).

By contrast, subjective weights for confidence or perceived relative expertise, by the estimators or by their peers, notably do *not* improve the accuracy of the weighted average estimates. Both prediction markets and Delphi methods produced improvements over the performance of typical individuals. Somewhat surprisingly, the most successful judgment aid was a good old-fashioned chat room with an unregulated discussion of current forecast problems (pursued by the Good Judgment Team, led by Barbara Mellers and Philip Tetlock at the University of Pennsylvania).

As we see it, the early results from the forecasting tournament are reassuring insofar as they tend to reinforce the principal lessons we have presented here. But in one respect, we are a little disappointed. To date, the tournament has mostly produced methods that improve decisions by removing some of usual noise and bias from a forecast. What we really want to see are game-changing methods that don't just reduce noise, but also amplify the signal. As yet, the tournament has not led to such benefits, which are likely to derive from more-effective information-pooling.

A lot remains to be learned, but carefully conducted face-to-face or structured deliberations might be effective in this regard. For example, an enhanced Delphi method, in which forecasters or decision makers are trained to pool unshared information, thereby escaping hidden profiles and the common-knowledge trap, could lead to breakthroughs, not just to incremental improvements. A lot more work would be necessary to demonstrate that our conjecture is correct. But in this context at least, there is little harm in trying.

The Forest

The topic of tournaments is fascinating and important, and it deserves a whole book of its own. But let's focus on the forest and not get lost in the trees.

First, tournaments are an excellent way to reduce group failures, because they can overcome the problems explored in the first part of this book. Second, many institutions, both small and large, should be experimenting with tournaments to see if they can spark creativity. And finally, it often makes sense to go outside your own institution and to create incentives to get a little help, and maybe a lot of it, from outsiders. If you ask the whole world, you might be surprised and excited by what you learn.

11

Prediction Markets

Prediction markets, a recent innovation, have proved remarkably successful at forecasting events. Indeed, such markets often
seem to do better than deliberating groups. Prediction markets are
worth careful attention because they offer important insights into
how to make deliberation go better, because they provide general
lessons about collective intelligence, and because an actual prediction market can sometimes be a useful device for many private and
public organizations.

Hayek and the Price System

To understand prediction markets, we should begin with Friedrich Hayek, the great twentieth-century critic of socialism and
economic planning. Hayek emphasized the importance of free

markets, above all as a way of collecting and combining information. His most important contribution to social thought is captured in his great (and short) 1945 essay, "The Use of Knowledge in Society."[1]

In that essay, Hayek claims that the central advantage of prices is that they aggregate both the knowledge and the tastes of many people, incorporating far more information than could be assembled by any central planner, group, or board. Hayek emphasizes the unshared nature of information—the "dispersed bits of incomplete and frequently contradictory knowledge which all the separate individuals possess."[2] This knowledge certainly includes facts about products, but it also includes preferences and tastes, and all of these must be taken into account by a well-functioning market. Hayek stresses above all the "very important but unorganized knowledge which cannot possibly be called scientific in the sense of general rules: the knowledge of the particular circumstances of time and place."[3]

For Hayek, the key economic problem is how to incorporate that unorganized and dispersed knowledge. No one person or group can possibly solve that problem. Central planners cannot have access to all of the knowledge held by diverse people. Taken as a whole, the knowledge that they hold is far greater than that held by even the wisest and well-chosen group or experts. Whether or not Aristotle was right in his hopes for deliberation, Hayek shows that the possibility of surpassing the quality of the few best thinkers certainly does hold for free markets.

Hayek's central point is that if the problem is how to aggregate information, the best solution often comes from the price system. In a system in which knowledge of relevant facts is dispersed among many people, prices act as an astonishingly concise and accurate coordinating and signaling device. They incorporate dispersed knowledge and in a sense also broadcast it, because the price itself operates as a signal to all.

Even better, the price system has a wonderfully automatic quality, particularly in its ability to respond quickly to changes. If fresh information shows that a product—a television, a car, a tablet, a watch—doesn't work, people's demand for it will rapidly fall, and so too the price. And when a commodity suddenly becomes scarce, its users must respond to that event. In Hayek's account, the market works remarkably well as a whole, not because any participant can see all its features, but because the relevant information is communicated to everyone through prices.

Hence, Hayek claims that "[it] is more than a metaphor to describe the price system as a kind of machinery for registering changes, or a system of telecommunications which enables individual producers to watch merely the movement of a few pointers."[4] Hayek describes this process as a marvel and adds that he has chosen the word *marvel* on purpose so as "to shock the reader out of the complacency with which we often take the working of the mechanism for granted."[5] In Hayek's account, the price system is an extraordinary collective intelligence mechanism, partly because it collects what everyone knows and partly because it imposes the right incentives.

To be sure, there is a real question of whether Hayek was right or whether markets might also encode mistakes and confusion (as behavioral economists Robert Shiller, Richard Thaler, and others have emphasized).[6] In particular, Shiller argues that informational cascades and herd behavior affect stock prices, with investors following one another in a process of the blind leading the blind. In a fundamental challenge to Hayek's optimism about market processes, Shiller contends that "the same forces of human psychology that have driven the stock market over the years have the potential to affect other markets."[7]

We will return to the behavioral challenge—that markets can incorporate errors and illusions as easily as valid information—in a moment. For our purposes now, the central, practical question is this: Can people use the market mechanism to improve group judgments?

Incentives, Again

How might a company predict whether its own products will do well or poorly? A few years ago, Google adopted an innovative method.[8] The firm created a prediction market, in which its employees could place "bets" about a variety of outcomes of importance to the company. Participants made forecasts about when products would launch, their likely success, and many other prospects. They invested virtual money, which could be redeemed for various prizes. The investments, or bets, set a price. If, for example, most people believed that Google would sell two million units of a new product in the next year and they bet accordingly, the price would reflect that belief.

By and large, the outcomes of Google's prediction markets turned out to be stunningly accurate. If the price suggests that a product is likely to sell two million units, it is likely to sell two million units. If the price suggests that the product is not likely to launch by July 1, the product is unlikely to launch by that date. Dispersed knowledge within the company has been accurately aggregated in this way. Google's prediction markets have worked because many employees, with private information, have offered their own opinions, and the sum of those opinions, the market price, has usually been right. The most striking finding is that in prediction markets, prices generally have operated as probabilities.[9] When the price suggests that an event is 90 percent likely to happen, the event will happen 90 percent of the time.

Recall that in a deliberating group, members may have little incentive to say what they know. By speaking out, they provide benefits to others while possibly facing high private costs. By contrast, prediction markets realign incentives in a way that is precisely designed to overcome this problem. Because investments in such markets are generally not disclosed to employers (let alone the public), the bettors, or traders, need not fear any harm to their reputation if, for example, they have predicted that their own company's sales will be low or that a certain candidate, not much liked by their friends and colleagues, will be elected president.

Because participants stand to gain or lose from their investments, they have a strong incentive to use (and, in that sense, to disclose) whatever private information they hold. In fact, managers who have installed prediction markets tell us that the chat groups and information postings that accompany the market are as informative to the managers as the outputs of the markets themselves. And even if the details of the information remain private, it will be reflected in the price signal. In these crucial ways, the problems that afflict deliberating groups are largely eliminated in prediction markets.

Prediction markets also impose strong incentives for traders to ferret out accurate information. Traders are unlikely to trade blindly, and they are able to cease trading, for a moment or more, to seek better information that will give them an advantage. In many deliberating groups, by contrast, participants cannot leave; they must continue deliberating, and the necessary information is often dispersed and locked within individual participants.

Like everyone else, investors are, of course, subject to the informational pressure imposed by the views of others. But because people stand to gain from revealing (through investments or "bets") what they hold, a competitive market creates strong incentives for the revelation of whatever information people actually hold. And indeed, prediction markets have usually been found not to amplify individual errors but to eliminate them; the prices that result from trading prove reliable even if many individual traders err. In recent years, prediction markets have done more than just provide valuable information. In countless domains, their forecasts have proved extremely accurate, with prices generally operating as probabilities.

Some Successful Prediction Markets

Prediction markets, aggregating diverse views, are flourishing in numerous domains. Consider the Hollywood Stock Exchange, in which people predict (among many other things) Oscar nominees and winners as well as opening-weekend box-office figures. The level of accuracy has been impressive, especially considering the fact that the traders use virtual rather than real money.[10] Among the most noteworthy achievements of the exchange to date is its uncanny accuracy in predicting Oscar winners, with the most probable winner bringing home the Oscar in the overwhelming majority of categories for which trading has occurred. If you want to know who will be thanking the Academy, you will do quite well if you consult the Hollywood Stock Exchange. And in fact, prediction markets that use virtual money often do as well as markets that rely on real money.[11]

There are plenty of other examples. Many people believe that you can't predict the weather, but the National Weather Service does quite well, and orange juice futures do even better.[12] Another large prediction market focuses on the likelihood that economic data released later in the week will show specific values; the market has performed even better than the consensus forecasts of about fifty professional forecasters.[13]

Many companies are now using prediction markets to aggregate diverse views. Managers at the consumer electronics company Best Buy established a prediction market called TagTrade (named after the yellow tag in the company logo). In this market, employees can wager on the outcome of outside events (like presidential elections and sporting contests) and company events (like quarterly sales projections or whether a new branch would open on time). Although the market runs on token credits, participation is encouraged through prizes: the top investors receive a $200 gift certificate and, even more coveted, a special embroidered shirt.[14]

Remarkably, the TagTrade market has outperformed Best Buy's official sales team in forecasting quarterly results, has bested construction managers in predicting whether new offices would open on time, and has been credited with helping the company outlast longtime rival Circuit City.[15] By mid-2011, TagTrade had run 240 predictions and engaged twenty-one hundred of the company's US employees.[16]

A number of years ago, Hewlett-Packard (HP) and the California Institute of Technology initiated a project to study prediction markets as an information aggregation mechanism involving product sales.[17] The experimenters selected people who worked in different parts of HP's business operation. Because of its small size, the market was a very thin one, meaning that there were few participants and hence the market was far less liquid than ideal. Participants were chosen with the belief that each person could contribute information from his or her department.

The markets were organized so that securities existed for intervals of sales. For example, one security would pay off if sales were between one and ten printers; another would pay off if sales were between ten and twenty. In most of the experiments, the possible range of sales was divided into ten intervals of equal size. On the basis of the prices of each security, the experimenters could guess how many units HP would sell that month. Prediction markets were expected to have large advantages over internal projections that involve deliberation. Employees involved in sales have an incentive to understate projected outcomes, so as to ensure that the projections do not fall short of expectations; this bias, or a competing bias in favor of excessive optimism, can be reduced through market incentives.

The results showed that the markets' predictions were a real improvement over HP's official forecasts. In no fewer than six of the eight markets for which official forecasts were available, the market prediction was significantly closer to the actual outcome than the official forecast. Many other companies, including Ely Lilly and Company and Microsoft, have used prediction markets as well to supplement deliberation about future courses of action.

Since 1988, the University of Iowa has run the Iowa Electronic Markets (IEM), which allow people to bet on the outcome of presidential elections. Before the 2004 elections, the IEM did far better than professional polling organizations, outperforming polls 451 out of 596 times.[18] In the week before the four elections from 1988 to 2000, the predictions in the IEM showed an average absolute error of just 1.5 percent—a significant improvement over the 2.1 percent error in the final Gallup polls.[19] In 2004, the Iowa market did remarkably well. On midnight of November 1, it showed George W. Bush with 50.45 percent of the vote and John Kerry with 49.55 percent— very close to the final numbers of 51.56 percent for Bush and 48.44 percent for Kerry.

In 2008, the IEM predicted that Senator Joe Biden would be Senator Barack Obama's vice presidential nominee well before political commentators considered Biden the front-runner. In the hours before the nomination was announced, the IEM reflected an 80 percent likelihood that Biden would be the pick.[20] In 2008, the IEM offered a final prediction of Obama at 53.55 percent and McCain at 46.45 percent—very close to the ultimate tally of 52.93 and 45.65 percent, respectively. The IEM was similarly accurate during the 2012 presidential election than it was in 2008. The market's final forecast predicted 50.9 percent of the national vote for President Obama and 48.4 percent for Mitt Romney; the final tally was 50.6 percent for Obama, 47.8 percent for Romney.[21] Notably, the IEM has proved accurate not only on election eve but also in long forecasting horizons.[22]

Biases

What about biases? Might they affect prediction markets? Just as in group deliberation, investors in a market might be subject to predictable heuristics and biases. Of course, people are subject to these influences. For example, social scientists have found that people overestimate the likelihood that their own preferred candidate will win an election—a form of optimistic bias. At a certain point in the 1980 campaign, 87 percent of Jimmy Carter's supporters believed that he would win, while in the same election 80 percent of Ronald Reagan's supporters believed that their candidate would win.[23] Obviously, Carter's supporters greatly overestimated their candidate's probability of victory.

Is it shocking to hear that some gamblers in New York are particularly likely to bet on the New York Yankees?[24] IEM traders show the same bias. In 1988, Michael Dukakis supporters were more likely to hold IEM futures in the Massachusetts governor's ill-fated presidential bid than were supporters of George H. W. Bush.[25] More strikingly still, Dukakis supporters were more likely to view the candidates' debates as helpful to the Democratic candidate and accordingly bought significant additional futures in his campaign after each debate.[26] Supporters of Bush displayed precisely the same pattern.

People usually assimilate new information in a way that confirms their view of the world—confirmation bias—and those who invest in prediction markets show the same bias.[27] Undoubtedly, many investors lose money in the stock market for the same reason. In general, traders buy and sell in a way that fits with their party identification.[28]

Despite all this, the IEM proved extremely accurate, even more so than polls, in predicting the outcome of the 1988 presidential election. No less than three weeks before the election, the market provided an almost-perfect guess about the candidates' shares of the vote.[29] The simple finding is that while many people are biased, the markets as a whole are not. How is such accuracy possible when many traders are prone to blunder?

The likely answer lies in the *marginal-trader hypothesis*, which emphasizes the behavior of a small group of traders who are less susceptible to biases. According to this hypothesis, certain traders, immune to the major biases, have a disproportionately large effect on prices. In election markets, these traders have been able to earn significant profits at the expense of other traders.[30] If marginal traders are active and able to profit from the errors and biases of other participants, then there will be no effect on the aggregate market price—a real testimony to Hayek.

A distinct bias that might be expected to affect prediction markets is the *favorite-long-shot bias* often seen in horse races. In horse racing, heavy favorites tend to produce higher returns than do other horses in the field, whereas long shots tend to offer lower-than-expected returns.[31] The same bias is seen in tennis matches, where the best players get higher returns and the lower-ranked players attract a disproportionate share of bets.[32] In these domains, bettors undervalue near certainties and overvalue low probabilities.

If this point holds in general, prediction markets might not be accurate with respect to highly improbable events.[33] The market should be expected to overestimate the likelihood that such events will occur. But in existing prediction markets, we see at best modest evidence of systematic errors in this vein.[34]

In some markets, of course, biased traders do mean biased markets. The whole field of behavioral finance attempts to explain how biased markets can persist over time.[35] But prediction markets have generally been free from this problem. We will undoubtedly be learning a great deal more about this topic as it is an active area of research.

Bubbles and More

Everyone knows the stock market can contain bubbles, in which stocks trade well above their fundamental value. Bubbles often occur when people believe not that a stock is really worth a great deal, but that other people *think* that the stock is worth a great deal. Hence people invest with the expectation that value will increase because of the enthusiasm of other investors.[36]

Can bubbles occur in prediction markets? Of course they can. Prediction bubbles are easy to imagine, with investors moving in a certain direction with the belief that many other investors are doing the same. And if bubbles are possible, crashes are possible too.

In any case, informational influences can lead people to make foolish investments in any market, including those involving predictions. Informational cascades play a large role in investment decisions, just as in choices about what products to buy. A fad might suddenly benefit a sneaker company, a book, a television program, a restaurant, or a movie. Many people might be attracted to one of these, not because they have independent information that the product is good, or even because they believe that it is much better than the alternatives, but simply because they are following the signals provided by the cascade.

Hayek did not much grapple with the risk that markets will suffer from herd behavior. If he had, his best response would be that smart investors will be alert to that risk and willing to take advantage of it. If herds of people ensure that a product or a stock is a bargain, then other people—first a few, then a lot—will purchase it, and the market will eventually correct itself.

But experience shows that this view can be too optimistic, at least for ordinary stocks.[37] As prediction markets develop, significant individual errors should be expected and will undoubtedly produce some errors in the price signal. Consider the 2004 presidential election. On the day of the vote, dramatic news of pro-Kerry exit polls produced not only a huge switch in the conventional wisdom, but also a great deal of volatility in election markets, with a wild swing in the direction of Senator Kerry at the expense of President Bush.[38] The rumors affected investors, not just onlookers.

Large-scale errors are always possible when apparently relevant news leads numerous investors to buy or sell. Indeed, election day in 2004 may well have been a cascade, with investors responding to one another's judgments, even though the judgments were based on misleading information. But for those enthusiastic about prediction markets, there is some favorable evidence: the erroneous figures lasted only a few hours, after which the numbers returned to their previous level of accuracy.

Feasibility

For many groups, prediction markets face a pervasive problem of feasibility. They are not simple to create, and establishing them might prove confusing and time-consuming. If an employer or a local government needs to make a short-term decision, a prediction market is unlikely to make a lot of sense. When the relevant groups are small, effective markets may be impossible to create, simply because of the absence of sufficient numbers of investors. A certain number is necessary to ensure that prediction markets have enough information to aggregate. Nonetheless, some private and public institutions might well enlist such markets to resolve a number of questions, and ambitious efforts are under way to examine how public officials might use these markets.

In fact, governments might consider using prediction markets to help make projections about budget deficits, the risk of insolvency, and the probability of outbreaks of disease or natural disasters. In each of these cases, the results of prediction markets might provide a reality check on deliberative processes. Officials might take into account the markets' predictions of the anticipated damage from a natural disaster, the number of annual deaths from an actual or anticipated disease, and much more. In all these cases, private or public institutions might create markets to provide information on crucial questions, and public institutions might take that information into account in making judgments about policy.

12

Asking the Public

Every year, federal agencies issue thousands of new regulations. Whether the issue involves health care or immigration or clean air, federal policy is often made through rule making. Operating in groups, agencies try really hard to compile relevant information. We have noted that OIRA sees much of its responsibility as one of assembling dispersed information, so as to increase the likelihood that the relevant group—people who work for the government itself—is wiser.

But let's not celebrate too loudly. Public officials face a potentially serious problem—one that Hayek would certainly appreciate. Dedicated followers of Hayek call it the "knowledge problem." Even if public officials are expert, diverse, and well motivated, they may not know nearly enough. An air pollution regulation might have major effects on companies and on state and local governments all over the United States. The consequences of that regulation for Los Angeles, or for companies in Ohio and Utah and Michigan, might not be visible to regulators. The government may have terrific scientists (actually, it does), but there are a lot of scientists in the nation, and they often have information that government lacks. What can public officials do to obtain what they need to know?

A Little Law and a Big Surprise

Within the federal government, the answer goes by the name of notice-and-comment rule-making. Through this process, federal agencies send out proposed rules for notice and public comment and give people a reasonable period (at least sixty days) to comment. The rules might involve homeland security, air pollution, immigration, or food safety. Among professors of administrative law, there is a widespread cliché—let's call it the sophisticated view—to the effect that the comment process is a fraud, a charade, a form of kabuki theater. In the sophisticated view, the real work is done behind the scenes. When the proposed rule is presented to the public, it is essentially baked.

As Sunstein learned during his time in government, the sophisticated view turns out to be entirely wrong. On the contrary, the comment period greatly matters, and federal agencies take people's suggestions and concerns seriously. Such agencies do so for one reason above all: people have information that officials lack, and to get the rules right, officials need to take that information into account. Time and again, proposed rules are changed and significantly improved because of what various members of the public say in comments.

Sometimes the rules are clarified. Sometimes they are scaled back, because they would be too intrusive. Sometimes they are redirected, because the redirection makes them much better. Sometimes they are put on the back burner—and never appear again. The notice-and-comment approach is primarily a process of acquiring information, not of considering the threats of interest groups or playing politics.

This is the shortest chapter in this book, because the central idea is very simple. Drawing on current practice within the national government, we suggest that many other institutions, including private ones, might well benefit from some kind of notice-and-comment process, whether it is formal or informal. Suppose, for example, that a social media company is contemplating a change to its privacy policy. Might it not make sense for the company to take public comment? As one example, Facebook chose exactly this route, posting the following in August 2012:

> *We are proposing updates to our Data Use Policy and our Statement of Rights and Responsibilities. These two documents tell you about how we collect and use data, and the rules that apply when you choose to use Facebook. Please take a few minutes to read through the changes under the Documents tab, or below, and provide feedback within the next seven days. If your comments lead to more updates, we'll post those on this page, too.*

Of course, Facebook's privacy policy has not exactly been controversy-free, but an effort to seek public comment can have two benefits. First, it can increase the likelihood that the final decision will be well informed, simply because dispersed information will be collected. Second, it can increase goodwill and sense of legitimacy and fair play. In government, the public comment process gives people a sense that they have had a right to be heard. So long as that right is real, the final outcome is usually more acceptable than it would otherwise be, even if some people do not exactly love it on the merits. (True, face-to-face meetings are often better than a comment process, but such meetings can take a lot of time.) For the private sector, both of these benefits might be exceedingly important.

We can find many examples. The Network Advertising Initiative, a self-regulatory association of digital advertising companies, opted for a period of public comment before revising its code of conduct.[1] Similarly, a commercial real estate firm in Las Vegas sought advice from consumers about which kinds of tenants should fill various vacant retail spaces.[2] Each vacant unit sported a flyer declaring "Help! We Need Your Opinion!" and containing a unique QR code. Passersby could scan the code with their phones and offer feedback on what type of store would be most useful in that space.[3] Guns are not everybody's cup of tea, but Tracking-Point, a gun manufacturer, solicited public input on what type of firearm it should produce.[4] Or suppose a clothing company is considering a new product line. It might well benefit from seeking the dispersed information held by its actual and potential customers.

Certainly for the private sector, seeking public comment should not be the universal practice. There is a big difference between government and private firms. Companies are disciplined by the market, and they find out, pretty quickly, what people like and want to buy. Free markets depend on consumer reactions, and many companies do best to see what people actually choose, not to ask people for their comments in advance. If the goal is to learn whether products sell, actual behavior is a lot better than a survey.

Moreover, a public-comment period can also create risks, including a negative reaction from those whose comments are not ultimately heeded. We have said that public comment can improve the perceived legitimacy of ultimate decisions, but the whole enterprise might backfire.

Here as elsewhere, everything depends on costs and benefits, and the costs of requesting and using comments may exceed the benefits. But whenever an institution fears that its own judgment might be erroneous, it should consider the possibility of seeking feedback in advance. Sometimes that's the most generous thing to do, and sometimes it's good business to boot.

13

"One Ball"

In sports, some people are famous for "making other players better." Magic Johnson, the great basketball player and winner of five National Basketball Association (NBA) championships, was not merely a terrific scorer, passer, and rebounder; he also transformed his teammates—some of them ordinary players—into stars. Early in his career, Michael Jordan was known to be great, maybe even the greatest of the great, but his teams just didn't win. People wondered whether he could ever win a championship, because he "wasn't a team player."

In business, some people are thought to be like the young Michael Jordan—individual superstars who, apart from their own skills, don't add much to team efforts. But there are others, like Magic Johnson, who are widely thought to make others better. Is it possible to say something about what kind of person does that? Not something impressionistic, intuitive, and anecdotal, but something that is actually based on evidence? Intriguing answers are starting to emerge, and they involve something called Factor C.

Team Players

Social scientists have uncovered a statistical factor that reflects how people do on a large number of cognitive tasks; this factor is sometimes referred to as *general intelligence*. An obvious conclusion is that groups should seek people who have something like general intelligence. Indeed, that seems to be true. With respect to various measures of cognitive ability, there is a consistent finding across studies of many different small groups: groups with a higher average IQ tend to perform better.[1]

Interestingly, studies of actual work groups find a somewhat looser relationship than do studies of laboratory groups. But the evidence unequivocally shows that groups with smarter members perform at higher levels. This is not exactly a remarkable observation. But it is a good point to keep in mind when you're putting together a group of people.

There's an important qualification to this finding, and to identify it, we have to return to basketball. In 2010, the Miami Heat basketball team created a kind of dream team, with three genuine superstars: LeBron James, Dwayne Wade, and Chris Bosh. James and Wade rank among the best basketball players of all time, and Bosh has been an All-Star. When the team was initially assembled, Sunstein had the good fortune to meet the

Boston Celtics' Hall-of-Famer Bill Russell, who is the greatest winner, and the greatest team player, in the history of professional sports. In his thirteen years in the NBA, Russell won the championship eleven times—an astounding championship rate of 85 percent. By the way, Russell was an anxious leader. He was famous for vomiting before big games, and when he was in the bathroom (vomiting), his teammates knew that they could expect to win.

Excited and a bit terrified (what can one say to Bill Russell?), Sunstein asked Russell whether the Miami Heat would win the championship that year. Sunstein was confident that Russell would say yes; who could possibly beat a team with James, Wade, and Bosh? Instead Russell offered a definite "No!" When asked for an explanation, Russell gave a quiet but firm response: "One ball." And in fact, the Heat lost in the finals that year to the Dallas Mavericks, a far less skilled team—but a team.

Which brings us back to Michael Jordan. By the time he retired, Jordan had become one of the greatest all-time winners, besting Johnson (but not Russell) with six championships to his credit. What happened?

Here's a clue. Late in Game 5 of the 1991 NBA Finals at the Forum in Los Angeles, the Chicago Bulls were ahead 3 to 1 in the series, and they were clinging to a fragile lead. Though double-teamed, Jordan was still shooting a lot—and missing. During a crucial timeout, Phil Jackson, the Bulls' coach, looked Jordan right in the eyes and said, "Michael, who's open?" Michael didn't answer. Jackson asked again. "Michael, who's open?" Jordan responded: "Pax."

"Pax" was John Paxson, an unheralded guard who was a deadly shooter, at least when no one was covering him. Jordan got the ball to Paxson, who nailed a series of open shots. The Bulls claimed the first of their NBA championships. And by the way, the Miami Heat eventually became a team as well, winning two championships after its initial defeat, arguably because of improved teamwork.

Enough basketball. We have referred to Nancy-Ann DeParle and Jeff Zients, the anxious leaders in the Obama administration. They're very different, but they know there's just one ball, and they know who's open. Although they're worriers, they don't just admire problems; they see around the bend and hunt for solutions. DeParle and Zients know the importance of assembling teams, not simply on the basis of skill, but also on the basis of teamwork and the capacity to add what the group most needs.

Good players mesh. This observation may be a cliché, but it's nevertheless important to keep in mind: personalities—not merely abilities—matter. In this regard, most people's intuition, at least in Western cultures, would lead us to two conclusions. First, some personality types are far better than others (Bill Russell and Magic Johnson, as opposed to the early Michael Jordan). Second, successful groups have a good mixture of personality types.

Those observations are not exactly wrong, but they do not take us very far toward specifying the right mixture of personality types for a particular task. What kinds of personalities would be best able to figure out an investment strategy for next year? To decide how to market a cell phone? To conduct a negotiation to acquire a company? To invent a new pharmaceutical drug or execute an emergency evacuation? To figure out how to get a start-up off the ground? To plan a litigation strategy for a copyright case?

A Popular, Bad Answer

To answer such questions, by far the most popular choice in American companies has been the Myers-Briggs Type Indicator, a test that separates individuals into sixteen basic "types" based on their self-reports of life preferences. A lot of companies take the test seriously.

Before we explain why pigeonholing people into personality types is not a good idea in business, let's look at the general disadvantages of using personality assessments to predict behavior. Unlike members of more collectivist cultures (think Asia), Westerners seem obsessed with people's personality traits as a means of understanding and predicting future conduct. If we want to know what employee Smith will do under conditions of time pressure, we tend to ask ourselves, *What kind of person is Smith?* That isn't a crazy question, but in practice, even the most valid personality tests have only modest predictive power. Nonetheless, many people quite confidently rely on impressions of personality to explain the actions of their friends and colleagues.[2] Their confidence is often misplaced.

The problem is that we exaggerate how consistent people are across both situations and time. If someone is lazy around the house, we might conclude that he is also likely to be lazy at work or in the gym. If someone was easily distracted in class, he will also be easily distracted at work. But in many cases, this kind of cross-situational behavioral consistency does not exist. Most of us are a lot less consistent in how we behave in different situations than we think we are. This goes in spades for our beliefs about the consistency of other people. Relying on these mostly false beliefs about behavioral consistency and hence predictability, we are overconfident about how accurately we understand and can predict others.

Social psychologists call this tendency to rely excessively on personality descriptors, and to be overconfident in our capacities to predict behavior, the *fundamental attribution error*.[3] *Attribution* refers to everyday explanations that claim that other people's behavior is a product of a trait (e.g., extroversion, laziness) possessed by the actor. If even weakly valid traits, like extroversion and conscientiousness, have low predictive value, an unscientific trait categorization like the Myers–Briggs score is going to be totally useless for purposes of prediction or for designing a team or another collective.

Consider, for example, this question from the Myers–Briggs test: "Would you rather work under a boss (a) who is good-natured, but often inconsistent or (b) who is sharp-tongued, but always logical?" Your answer to this question is aimed to assign you to a "feeling" or a "thinking" category. Or consider this question: "Is it true (a) that facts 'speak for themselves' or (b) that facts 'illustrate principles'?" Your answer indicates whether you belong in the "perception" or "judging" category. Or this: "Are you the kind of person (a) who is external and communicative and likes to express yourself or (b) who is internal and reticent and keeps to yourself?" Your answer types you as extroverted or introverted. The sixteen Myers–Briggs types are defined by four dimensions: extroversion–introversion, sensing–intuition, thinking–feeling, and judging–perception.

By some reports, almost 90 percent of the major US companies use the Myers–Briggs test for employee selection, placement, or counseling.[4] But careful studies show that the test does not predict behavior of any kind with much validity.[5] One problem is that the test has what statisticians call low *test-retest reliability*. If you retake the test after a one-month gap, there's a 50 percent chance that you will fall into a different personality category from your original category. With such low reliability, the test is unlikely to have much predictive validity in companies that are deciding whether to assign an employee to a team for a three-month project.

One group of researchers, for example, studied the actual value of the Myers-Briggs test in teamwork applications and concluded that it "does not account for behavioral differences nor does it exactly clarify which characteristics of a particular function an individual may exhibit."[6] More generally, careful scientific reviews, including statistical meta-analyses, find little value in personality test scores, including scales that are more valid predictors of behavior than the Myers-Briggs.[7] It follows that the Myers-Briggs is not likely to provide guidance for managers trying to staff a team to perform a novel task.

At the same time, and the weakness of the Myers-Briggs notwithstanding, team performance does seem to depend on whether people are sociable in the relevant sense (a point for Bill Russell). More technically, research suggests that measures of preferences for social working conditions have provided fruitful clues for a successful team. Groups composed of people who prefer to work in teams do end up working better.[8] While the relationship between social preference and work success appears to be modest, it is real, and wise groups take it into account.

An Intriguing Finding

We need a lot more work on whether certain types are helpful to groups. But one especially thought-provoking development in recent research has been reported in studies from a group associated with the Center for Collective Intelligence at MIT.[9] These researchers wondered if there could be some general method to assess the problem-solving capacity of a team across many types of intellectual and social problems. They conducted two large-scale tests of two- to five-member groups, solving problems such as brainstorming, answering IQ test questions, solving moral dilemmas, and even playing checkers.

Their central finding is that three individual-member measures combined into a useful measure of collective IQ, which the researchers called Factor C. First, the average of the members' scores on a test of social perception (the Reading the Mind in the Eyes Test) predicted performance: the higher the average, the higher the group's performance. This test was originally invented by the psychologist Simon Baron-Cohen (brother of the actor and comic Sacha Baron-Cohen) to diagnose autism in children.[10] The person taking the test is shown a series of photos of just the eyes of another person and asked to judge what emotion the person in the photo is experiencing (e.g., playful, irritated, bored).

The second measure, unevenness of participation, or the tendency of a few members to dominate a discussion, was negatively related to group performance. Intriguingly, the third measure, the number of women on the team, positively predicted performance.

Perhaps the most striking conclusion is that the Factor C measure predicted team performance better than conventional measures of intelligence did. (Compare the 2010 Dallas Mavericks, consisting of team players, to the star-studded 2010 Miami Heat.) Average IQ and highest IQ were not correlated with team performance nearly as highly as Factor C. More technically, IQ measures were correlated in the +.10 to +.20 range; Factor C was correlated at the high level of +.50 (+1.00 is the highest possible correlation).

The other noteworthy result was the simple, direct relationship between the percentage of women members and performance. This correlation was not simply a diversity factor; rather, the more women, the better the performance. Other research supports this basic finding.[11] But we should be pretty careful here, because the finding may be explained by the observation that women are also consistently better than men at a variety of social perception and social judgment tests (like the Reading the Mind in the Eyes Test used in these studies).

With respect to Factor C, Nancy-Ann DeParle and Jeff Zients are superstars. DeParle can size up a room, and a person, in an instant. She can take its emotional temperature, see behind the happy talk, and supply exactly what's needed. And within Sunstein's first month at the White House, a (female) friend of his said, with a combination of incredulity and admiration, that Jeff Zients "has the most emotional intelligence of any man I've ever met." At the time, Zients was a newcomer to government, and he had a ton to learn. But he had already mastered something very much like Factor C.

To be sure, we should be careful to avoid extravagant conclusions here. At this stage, it is difficult to identify exactly what underlies the high correlation between Factor C and performance on the problem-solving tasks. What seems to be the most important is the capacity of the individual members to cooperate with one another and to coordinate their performance. Unfortunately, it is always difficult to define the true causal factor in correlations of this type.

Nonetheless, the finding does suggest an important direction for research on whether particular individuals are especially good (other things being equal) at contributing to group performance.

Take that possibility seriously and, by analogy with research on individual performance, see if a general, quantifiable measure of Factor C can be defined. Such a measure would be extremely valuable in allowing us to design groups that are more effective. It would also stimulate further research on the nature of the effective ingredient captured at least partly by Factor C.

Beyond the institutional recommendations made here, wise groups should devote real attention to social abilities, including the capacities both to participate and to listen, in selecting personnel and in devising social norms. A person's preference to work on teams, especially when the preference is linked to social skills, is a good predictor—as is the ability to read other people's emotional states.

Face-to-Face versus Online

But when, exactly, will Factor C really matter? Some groups have a lot of members who operate independently. Some of these members have little emotional intelligence, and in the usual respects, you wouldn't consider them team players. Maybe they're a bit autistic. But they're sensational at their individual jobs, and the groups are a lot better because of them. Most groups have members and even leaders like that. (Steve Jobs was not exactly famous for his emotional intelligence.) Why aren't they a problem?

It is important to make a distinction that cuts across many types of collectives (teams, committees, electronic crowds, and so forth). Some team members act wholly or somewhat independently to complete the task. Other team members have to coordinate, perhaps even at the lowest levels of work, on that task. In terms of evaluating the importance of personality, the difference greatly matters.

Many tasks can be "crowdsourced," in the sense that individuals can work on their contributions independently until the ultimate stage in the task requires integrating or selecting a contribution. This is true in many forecasting tasks ("take an average"), tournaments (everyone suggests his or her individual best solutions and anyone can see which solution is the best), elections (each voter seeks out some information, perhaps with social deliberation, and then submits a vote or conclusion independently). In other cases, ingenious aggregation devices (prediction markets) integrate individual, independent solutions into a collective answer.

By contrast, many collective endeavors require coordination from the beginning to the end. The most obvious example is the classic face-to-face, physically connected team that must combine interdependent pieces and adjust them repeatedly to make them fit together into a functioning whole. (By the way, there is a lot of interest these days in the idea of telecommuting, which can make work a lot better for a lot of people, especially if they have young children. And if coordination is not required, telecommuting should be just fine. But when face-to-face interaction is needed—and it often is—telecommuting comes with a real cost. For overall productivity, the record of telecommuting is mixed.)

Consider a team constructing a physical product—say, a bridge, a ship, or an entrée. The members must interact frequently and with quick, coordinated responses, or the product risks falling apart. Many less tangible "products" also require more coordination and real-time interaction. For example, the development of a litigating position within a law firm may well require continuing discussions, and if people are trying to create a new tablet or computer, it is probably best if they work with one another.

What is remarkable about the rise of electronic networks is how many tasks that seemed to require face-to-face, real-time collaboration can be performed with much less coordination over networks. The game-changing example is software coding, which seemed to demand face-to-face teamwork until landmark projects like the open-source operating system Linux were developed.

Before 1992, there were many efforts to create distributed software systems to support the collaborative development of computer programs. Many commercial programs were written online, with loosely synchronized team processes. But in 1991, Linus Torvalds took this method to the next level when he invited thousands of programmers to contribute to his operating system and shifted the coordination to a late-stage selection and editing process, instead of an early-stage guidance role.[12] Obviously, *Wikipedia* is another example of a new method of collaborating, where identification occurs mostly in a wide-open, early stage and where coordination and integration only occur very late in the process in a selection and editing stage.[13]

All this is to say that social skills and an appetite for working on teams may not be essential in every kind of successful collective, especially those that do not require a face-to-face, real-time process. Extreme independence may even be a plus. But if the team process requires coordination in early stages or throughout the process, then Factor C and other aspects of sociability will matter a great deal. There may be only one ball, but whether that's a problem depends on the nature of the task that the group is asked to complete.

The Bright Future

For identifiable reasons, groups often perform poorly. In some cases, groups do not merely fail to correct the errors of their members; they actually amplify those errors. In this way, the behavioral biases displayed by individuals are replicated, and often even aggravated, within groups. It's a big mistake to think that when a group's individual members are prone to error, the group as a whole will correct those errors.

Wise groups and their leaders are constantly alert to these risks and attempt to change people's incentives. They do not ask for happy talk. Smart leaders are anxious. They help to elicit information by silencing themselves and by allowing other group members to talk, even if those members have low status. If a group's members are asked to adopt certain roles (formally or informally), information is far less likely to get lost. As we have noted, the idea of "equities," often invoked within the federal government, increases the likelihood that groups will obtain the information they need.

Wise leaders embrace a particular idea of what it means to be a team player: not to agree with the majority's current view, but to add valuable information. Leaders create a culture that does not punish, and even rewards, the expression of dissident views. They do so to protect not the dissident, but the group. Groups can take steps to combine statistical averaging with deliberation, perhaps by ensuring that people's private views are expressed and recorded before discussion begins.

For the future, some of the most promising innovations are supported by modern technologies. Tournaments can be created quickly, almost immediately, and they can engage many competitors, some of whom will have helpful or even amazing ideas. Prediction markets often work, because they create the right incentives. With some kind of process for public comment, both private and public groups obtain information from countless people with whom they do not and cannot directly interact. And if groups seek to develop new options, and not merely to select among existing ones, they have a host of available strategies. With new technologies, the sky may not be the limit.

The failures of groups often have disastrous consequences—not just for group members, but for all those who are affected by those failures. The good news is that decades of empirical work, alongside recent innovations, offer a toolbox of practical safeguards, correctives, and enhancements. With a few identifiable steps, groups can get a lot wiser.

Notes

Introduction

1. See Daniel Kahneman, *Thinking, Fast and Slow* (New York: Farrar, Straus and Giroux, 2011).

2. Aristotle, *Politics*, trans. E. Barker (London: Oxford University Press, 1972), 123.

3. John Rawls, *A Theory of Justice* (Cambridge: Belknap Press, 1971), 358–359.

4. Irving L. Janis, *Groupthink*, 2nd ed. (Boston: Houghton Mifflin, 1982), 7–9.

5. For an overview, see Marlene E. Turner, Anthony R. Pratkanis, and Christina K. Struckman, "Groupthink As Social Identity Maintenance," in *The Science of Social Influence: Advances and Future Progress*, ed. Anthony Pratkanis (New York: Psychology Press, 2007), 223–246.

6. Ibid.

7. Kahneman, *Thinking Fast and Slow*; Dan Ariely, *Predictably Irrational: The Hidden Forces That Shape Our Decisions* (New York: Harper, 2008); Sendhil Mullainathan and Eldar Shafir, *Scarcity: Why Having Too Little Means So Much* (New York: Times Books, Henry Holt and Company, 2013); Richard H. Thaler and Cass R. Sunstein, *Nudge: Improving Decisions About Health, Wealth, and Happiness* (New York: Penguin, 2009).

Chapter 1

1. Chip Heath and Rich Gonzalez, "Interaction with Others Increases Decision Confidence but Not Decision Quality: Evidence Against Information Collection Views of Interactive Decision Making," *Organizational Behavior and Human Decision Processes* 61 (1995): 305–326.

2. See Robert S. Baron et al., "Social Corroboration and Opinion Extremity," *Journal of Experimental Social Psychology* 32 (1996): 537–560.

3. Huaye Li and Yasuaki Sakamoto, "The Influence of Collective Opinion on True-False Judgment and Information-Sharing Decision," unpublished manuscript, February 1, 2013, http://ssrn.com/abstract=2210742.

4. Ibid.

5. Robert L. Thorndike, "The Effect of Discussion upon the Correctness of Group Decisions: When the Factor of Majority Influence Is Allowed For," *Journal of Social Psychology* 9 (1938): 343–362.

6. Daniel Gigone and Reid Hastie, "Proper Analysis of the Accuracy of Group Judgments," *Psychological Bulletin* 121 (1997): 149, 161; Reid Hastie, "Review Essay: Experimental Evidence on Group Accuracy," in *Information Pooling and Group Decision Making*, ed. Bernard Grofman and Guillermo Owen (Greenwich, CT: JAI Press, 1986), 129–158.

7. Robert J. MacCoun, "Comparing Micro and Macro Rationality," in *Judgments, Decisions, and Public Policy*, ed. Rajeev Gowda and Jeffrey Fox (Cambridge: Cambridge University Press, 2002), 116, 121.

8. J. Scott Armstrong, "Combining Forecasts," in *Principles of Forecasting: A Handbook for Researchers and Practitioners*, ed. J. Scott Armstrong (New York: Springer, 2001), 433.

9. James Surowiecki, *The Wisdom of Crowds: Why the Many Are Smarter than the Few and How Collective Wisdom Shapes Business, Economies, Societies, and Nations* (New York: Doubleday, 2004).

10. Irving Lorge et al., "A Survey of Studies Contrasting the Quality of Group Performance and Individual Performance, 1920–1957," *Psychological Bulletin* 55 (1958): 344.

11. Surowiecki, *The Wisdom of Crowds*, 5 (discussing jar experiment).

12. Ibid., xi–xiii.

13. Some affirmative evidence can be found in Armstrong, "Combining Forecasts," 417, 419–420, 427, 433–435.

14. Ibid., 16.

15. Theodore C. Sorensen, *Kennedy* (New York: Harper & Row, 1965), 306.

16. Arthur M. Schlesinger Jr., *A Thousand Days: John F. Kennedy in the White House* (New York: Houghton Mifflin, 1965), 258–259.

17. Ibid., 255.

18. See the overview in Solomon E. Asch, "Opinions and Social Pressure," in *Readings About the Social Animal*, 11th ed., ed. Joshua Aronson and Elliott Aronson (New York: Worth, 2011), 17–26.

19. Reid Hastie, Steven Penrod, and Nancy Pennington, *Inside the Jury* (Cambridge, MA: Harvard University Press, 1983).

20. Caryn Christensen and Ann S. Abbott, "Team Medical Decision Making," in *Decision Making in Health Care*, ed. Gretchen B. Chapman and Frank A. Sonnenberg (New York: Cambridge University Press, 2000), 267, 273–276.

Chapter 2

1. For an overview, see Thomas Gilovich, Dale Griffin, and Daniel Kahneman, *Heuristics and Biases: The Psychology of Intuitive Judgment* (New York: Cambridge University Press, 2002).

2. Amos Tversky and Daniel Kahneman, "Availability: A Heuristic for Judging Frequency and Probability," *Cognitive Psychology* 5 (1973): 208.

3. Paul Slovic, *The Perception of Risk* (London: Earthscan Publications, 2000), 37–48.

4. Ibid., 40.

5. Amos Tversky and Daniel Kahneman, "Judgment Under Uncertainty: Heuristics and Biases," in *Judgment Under Uncertainty: Heuristics and Biases*, ed. Daniel Kahneman, Paul Slovic, and Amos Tversky (Cambridge: Cambridge University Press, 1982), 3.

6. Daniel Kahneman and Shane Frederick, "Representativeness Revisited: Attribute Substitution in Intuitive Judgment," in *Heuristics and Biases: The Psychology of Intuitive Judgment*, ed. Thomas Gilovich, Dale W. Griffin, and Daniel Kahneman (Cambridge: Cambridge University Press, 2002), 49.

7. Paul Rozin and Carol Nemeroff, "Sympathetic Magical Thinking: The Contagion and Similarity 'Heuristics,'" in *Heuristics and Biases*, Gilovich, Griffin, and Kahneman, eds., 201.

8. Malcolm Gladwell, *Blink: The Power of Thinking Without Thinking* (New York: Little, Brown, and Co., 2005).

9. Alexander Todorov, Anesu N. Mandisodza, Amir Goren, and Crystal C. Hall, "Inferences of Competence from Faces Predict Election Results," *Science Magazine* 308 (2005): 1623–1626.

10. An excellent set of summaries of various biases can be found in *Cognitive Illusions*, Rüdiger F. Pohl, ed., (New York: Psychology Press, 2012).

11. Don Moore, Elizabeth Tenney, and Uriel Haran, "Overprecision in Judgment," in *Blackwell Handbook of Judgment and Decision Making*, ed. Gideon Keren and George Wu (Oxford: Blackwell, forthcoming).

12. Roger Buehler, Dale Griffin, and Johanna Peetz, "The Planning Fallacy: Cognitive, Motivational, and Social Origins," *Advances in Experimental Social Psychology* 43 (2010): 1.

13. Scott A. Hawkins and Reid Hastie, "Hindsight: Biased Judgments of Past Events After the Outcomes Are Known," *Psychological Bulletin* 107 (1990): 311–327.

14. Hal R. Arkes and Catherine Blumer, "The Psychology of Sunk Cost," *Organizational Behavior and Human Decision Processes* 35 (1985): 124–140.

15. Garold Stasser and Beth Dietz-Uhler, "Collective Choice, Judgment, and Problem Solving," in *Blackwell Handbook of Group Psychology: Group Processes*, ed. Michael A. Hogg and R. Scott Tindale (Oxford: Blackwell, 2001), 48.

16. Ibid.

17. Janet A. Sniezek and Rebecca A. Henry, "Accuracy and Confidence in Group Judgment," *Organizational Behavior and Human Decision Processes* 43 (1989): 1–28. This finding very much bears on excessive risk-taking, including in the context of making war. See Dominic Johnson, *Overconfidence and War: The Havoc and Glory of Positive Illusions* (Cambridge, MA: Harvard University Press, 2004), 180–183.

18. See Norbert L. Kerr, Robert J. MacCoun, and Geoffrey P. Kramer, "Bias in Judgment: Comparing Individuals and Groups," *Psychology Review* 103 (1996): 687, 689, 691–693.

19. Edward L. Schumann and W. C. Thompson, "Effects of Attorney's Arguments on Jurors' Use of Statistical Evidence," unpublished manuscript, 1989.

20. Glen Whyte, "Escalating Commitment in Individual and Group Decision Making: A Prospect Theory Approach," *Organizational Behavior and Human Decision Processes* 54 (1993): 430.

21. Ibid., 430–455.

22. Robert J. MacCoun, "Comparing Micro and Macro Rationality," in *Judgments, Decisions, and Public Policy*, ed. Rajeev Gowda and Jeffrey Fox (Cambridge: Cambridge University Press, 2002), 116, 121.

23. Mark F. Stasson et al., "Group Consensus Processes on Cognitive Bias Tasks: A Social Decision Scheme Approach," *Japanese Psychological Research* 30 (1988): 68–77.

24. See generally Dagmar Stahlberg et al., "We Knew It All Along: Hindsight Bias in Groups," *Organizational Behavior and Human Decision Processes* 63 (1995): 46–58.

Chapter 3

1. A. N. Meltzoff and K. Moore, "Imitation of Facial and Manual Gestures by Human Neonates," *Science* 198 (1977): 75–78; and see G. Rizzolatti and L. Craighero, "The Mirror-Neuron System," *Annual Review of Neuroscience* 27 (2004): 169–192.

2. Elaine Hatfield, John T. Caccioppo, and R. L. Rapson, *Emotional Contagion* (New York: Cambridge University Press, 1994); Nicholas A. Christakis and J. H. Fowler, "The Spread of Obesity in a Large Social Network over 32

Years," *New England Journal of Medicine* 357 (2007): 370–379; J. H. Fowler and Nicholas A. Christakis, "Dynamic Spread of Happiness in a Large Social Network: Longitudinal Analysis over 20 Years in the Framingham Heart Study," *British Medical Journal* 337 (2008): 1–9.

3. Matthew J. Salganik, Peter Sheridan Dodds, and Duncan J. Watts, "Experimental Study of Inequality and Unpredictability in an Artificial Cultural Market," *Science* 311 (2006): 854–856; Matthew Salganik and Duncan Watts, "Leading the Herd Astray: An Experimental Study of Self-fulfilling Prophecies in an Artificial Cultural Market," *Social Psychology Quarterly* 71 (2008): 338–355; Matthew Salganik and Duncan Watts, "Web-Based Experiments for the Study of Collective Social Dynamics in Cultural Markets," *Topics in Cognitive Science* 1 (2009): 439–468.

4. Salganik and Watts, "Leading the Herd Astray."

5. Jan Lorenz et al., "How Social Influences Can Undermine the Wisdom of Crowd Effect," *Proceedings of National Academy of Sciences* 108 (2011): 9020–9025.

6. This is a "soft" result, as the conclusion depends on the statistics used to analyze the data, but overall, groups were still wiser than individuals, though not always at conventional levels of statistical significance; Barbara Mellers, Wharton School, interview with authors, Philadelphia, August 14, 2013.

7. The literature here is vast. For a superb summary, see David Hirschleifer, "The Blind Leading the Blind," in *The New Economics of Human Behavior,* ed. Marianno Tommasi and Kathryn Ierulli (Cambridge: Cambridge University Press, 1995), 188.

8. We draw here on Hirschleifer, "The Blind Leading the Blind," 188, 193–194.

9. For a theoretical discussion, see Erik Eyster and Matthew Rabin, "Naïve Herding in Rich-Information Settings," *American Economic Journal: Microeconomics* 2 (2010): 221–243.

10. Judith M. Punchoar and Paul W. Fox, "Confidence in Individual and Group Decision Making: When 'Two Heads' Are Worse Than One," *Journal of Educational Psychology* 96 (2004): 582–591.

11. Cameron Anderson and Gavin J. Kilduff, "Why Do Dominant Personalities Attain Influence in Face-to-Face Groups? The Competence-Signaling Effects of Trait Dominance," *Journal of Personality and Social Psychology* 96 (2009): 491–503; Sunita Sah, Don A. Moore, and Robert J. MacCoun, "Cheap Talk and Credibility: The Consequences of Confidence and Accuracy on Advisor Credibility and Persuasiveness," *Organizational Behavior and Human Decision Processes* 121 (2013): 246–255.

12. Ibid.; Cass R. Sunstein, *Why Societies Need Dissent* (Cambridge, MA: Harvard University Press, 2003).

13. Lisa R. Anderson and Charles A. Holt, "Information Cascades in the Laboratory," *American Economic Review* 87 (1997): 847–862.

14. Angela A. Hung and Charles R. Plott, "Information Cascades: Replication and an Extension to Majority Rule and Conformity-Rewarding Institutions," *American Economic Review* 91 (2001): 1508, 1515.

15. Thus, 72 percent of subjects followed Bayes's rule in Anderson and Holt, "Information Cascades in the Laboratory," and 64 percent in Marc Willinger and Anthony Ziegelmeyer, "Are More Informed Agents Able to Shatter Information Cascades in the Lab?" in *The Economics of Networks: Interaction and Behaviours*, ed. Patrick Cohendet et al. (New York: Springer, 1998), 291, 304.

16. Willinger and Ziegelmeyer, "Are More Informed Agents," 291.

17. Anderson and Holt, "Information Cascades in the Laboratory," 847.

18. Jacob K. Goeree, Thomas R. Palfrey, Brian W. Rogers, and Richard D. McKelvey, "Self-Correcting Information Cascades," *Review of Economic Studies* 74 (2007): 733–762, found that when chains were longer than twenty members, the groups tended to correct themselves.

19. Hung and Plott, "Information Cascades," 1515–1517.

20. Ibid., 1516.

21. Timur Kuran and Cass R. Sunstein, "Availability Cascades and Risk Regulation," *Stanford Law Review* 51 (1988): 683–768.

22. Robert E. Kennedy, "Strategy Fads and Competitive Convergence: An Empirical Test for Herd Behavior in Prime-Time Television Programming," *Journal of Industrial Economics* 50 (2002): 57–84.

Chapter 4

1. Roger Brown, *Social Psychology: The Second Edition* (New York: Free Press, 1986), 206–207.

2. Ibid., 204.

3. Ibid., 224.

4. For a clear discussion, see ibid.

5. Serge Moscovici and Marisa Zavalloni, "The Group as a Polarizer of Attitudes," *Journal of Personality and Social Psychology* 12 (1969): 125–135.

6. Ibid.

7. Ibid.

8. Cass R. Sunstein et al., *Are Judges Political? An Empirical Investigation of the Federal Judiciary* (Washington, DC: Brookings Institution Press, 2006).

9. David Schkade, Cass R. Sunstein, and Daniel Kahneman, "Deliberating About Dollars: The Severity Shift," *Columbia Law Review* 100 (2000): 1139.

10. Brown, *Social Psychology*, 200–245. An effort to systematize some of these points can be found in Edward L. Glaeser and Cass R. Sunstein, "Extremism and Social Learning," *Journal of Legal Analysis* 1 (2009): 263–324.

11. Brown, *Social Psychology*. It has similarly been suggested that majorities are especially potent because people do not want to incur the wrath or otherwise lose the favor of large numbers of others, and that when minorities have influence, it is because they produce genuine attitudinal change. See Robert S. Baron et al., "Social Corroboration and Opinion Extremity," *Journal of Experimental Social Psychology* 32 (1996): 82.

12. Baron et al., "Social Corroboration," 557–559, shows that corroboration increases confidence and hence extremism.

13. Ibid., 541, 546–547, 557, concludes that corroboration of one's views has effects on opinion extremity.

14. Brown, *Social Psychology*, 209–211; John C. Turner, Margaret S. Wetherell, and Michael A. Hogg, "Referent Informational Influence and Group Polarization," *British Journal of Social Psychology* 28 (1989): 135–147; Joel Cooper, Kimberly A. Kelly, and Kimberlee Weaver, "Attitudes, Norms, and Social Groups," in *Social Cognition*, ed. Marilynn B. Brewer and Miles Hewstone (Oxford: Blackwell, 2004), 259, 269–270.

15. Brown, *Social Psychology*, 210.

16. Alex Pentland, *Social Physics: How Good Ideas Spread—The Lessons from A New Science* (New York: Penguin, 2014).

17. Brown, *Social Psychology*, 211; Cooper, Kelly, and Weaver, "Attitudes, Norms and Social Groups," 269.

18. Brendan Nyhan, Jason Reifler, and Peter Ubel, "The Hazards of Correcting Myths About Health Care Reform," *Medical Care* 51 (2013): 127–132.

19. Brooke Harrington, *Pop Finance: Investment Clubs and the New Investor Populism* (Princeton, NJ: Princeton University Press, 2008).

Chapter 5

1. Garold Stasser and William Titus, "Hidden Profiles: A Brief History," *Psychological Inquiry* 14 (2003): 304–313.

2. Daniel Gigone and Reid Hastie, "The Common Knowledge Effect: Information Sharing and Group Judgment," *Journal of Personality and Social Psychology* 65 (1993): 959–974.

3. Ross Hightower and Lutfus Sayeed, "The Impact of Computer-Mediated Communication Systems on Biased Group Discussion," *Computers in Human Behavior* 11 (1995): 33–44.

4. Patricia Wallace, *The Psychology of the Internet* (Cambridge: Cambridge University Press, 1999), 82.

5. Garold Stasser and William Titus, "Pooling of Unshared Information in Group Decision Making: Biased Information Sampling During Discussion," *Journal of Personality and Social Psychology* 48 (1985): 1467–1478.

6. Ibid., 1473; see also Stasser and Titus, "Hidden Profiles," 304.

7. Stasser and Titus, "Pooling of Unshared Information," 1473.

8. Ibid., 1476.

9. Ibid.

10. Ibid.

11. Stasser and Titus, "Hidden Profiles," 305.

12. Daniel Gigone and Reid Hastie, "The Common Knowledge Effect."

13. Ibid., 960.

14. Ibid., 973.

15. Ibid.

16. Susanne Abel, Garold Stasser, and Sandra I. Vaughan-Parsons, "Information Sharing and Cognitive Centrality," paper ERS-2005-037 (Rotterdam: Erasmus Research Institute of Management, May 2005).

17. Tatsuya Kameda, Yohsuke Ohtsubo, and Masanori Takezawa, "Centrality in Sociocognitive Networks and Social Influence: An Illustration in a Group Decision-Making Context," *Journal of Personality and Social Psychology* 73 (1997): 296–309.

18. Garold Stasser, Laurie A. Taylor, and Coleen Hanna, "Information Sampling in Structured and Unstructured Discussions of Three- and Six-Person Groups," *Journal of Personality and Social Psychology* 57 (1989): 67, 72–73.

19. Ibid., 78.

20. Ibid; though high-status members also "self-censor" (Melissa C. Thomas-Hunt, Tonya Y. Ogden, and Margaret A. Neale, "Who's Really Sharing? Effects of Social Expert Status on Knowledge Exchange Within Groups," *Management Science* 49 [2003]: 464–477).

21. Cecilia L. Ridgeway, "Social Status and Group Structure," in *Blackwell Handbook of Group Psychology: Group Processes*, ed. Michael A. Hogg and R. Scott Tindale (Oxford: Blackwell, 2001), 352, 354 (collecting studies).

22. Gwen M. Wittenbaum, Anne P. Hubbell, and Cynthia Zuckerman, "Mutual Enhancement: Toward an Understanding of the Collective

Preference for Shared Information," *Journal of Personality and Social Psychology* 77 (1999): 967, 967–978.

23. Stasser and Titus, "Hidden Profiles," 311.

Chapter 6

1. Carsten K. W. De Dreu, "Minority Dissent, Attitude Change, and Group Performance," in *The Science of Social Influence: Advances and Future Progress*, ed. Anthony R. Pratkanis (New York: Psychology Press, 2007), 247–270.

2. Ibid.

3. Caryn Christensen and Ann S. Abbott, "Team Medical Decision Making," in *Decision Making in Health Care*, ed. Gretchen B. Chapman and Frank A. Sonnenberg (New York: Cambridge University Press, 2000), 272–276.

4. Ibid; and also consider Sheryl Sandberg, *Lean In: Women, Work, and the Will to Lead* (New York: Knopf, 2013).

5. Cecilia L. Ridgeway, "Social Status and Group Structure," in *Blackwell Handbook of Group Psychology: Group Processes*, ed. Michael A. Hogg and R. Scott Tindale (Oxford: Blackwell, 2001), 354.

6. Harry Kalven and Hans Zeisel, *The American Jury* (Boston: Little Brown, 1966).

7. Garold Stasser and William Titus, "Hidden Profiles: A Brief History," *Psychological Inquiry* 14 (2003): 308.

8. Ibid.

9. Varda Liberman, Steven M. Samuels, and Lee Ross, "The Name of the Game: Predictive Power of Reputations Versus Situational Labels in Determining Prisoner's Dilemma Game Moves," *Personality and Social Psychology Bulletin*, 30 (2004): 1175–1185.

10. Stasser and Titus, "Hidden Profiles," 309.

11. Jeffrey A. Sonnenfeld, "What Makes Great Boards Great," *Harvard Business Review*, September 2002, http://hbr.org/2002/09/what-makes-great-boards-great/.

12. Brooke Harrington, *Pop Finance: Investment Clubs and the New Investor Populism* (Princeton, NJ: Princeton University Press, 2008).

13. Angela A. Hung and Charles R. Plott, "Information Cascades: Replication and an Extension to Majority Rule and Conformity-Rewarding Institutions," *American Economic Review* 91 (2001): 1515.

14. Garold Stasser, "The Uncertain Role of Unshared Information in Collective Choice," in *Shared Cognition in Organization: The Management of*

Knowledge, ed. Leigh L. Thompson, John M. Levine, and David M. Messick (Mahwah, NJ: Erlbaum, 1999): 49, 56–57.

15. Stasser and Titus, "Hidden Profiles," 308 (citing studies showing that "when the bearer of unique information was labeled an expert, the group seemingly paid more attention to the information"); Garold Stasser, Dennis D. Stewart, and Gwen M. Wittenbaum, "Expert Roles and Information Exchange During Discussion: The Importance of Knowing Who Knows What," *Journal of Experimental Social Psychology* 31 (1995): 244, 248–249, 256 (showing that assigning expert roles led to more discussion of unshared data).

16. Stasser, Stewart, and Wittenbaum, "Expert Roles," 248–249.

17. The tale is well told in Marlene E. Turner et al., "Groupthink As Social Identity Maintenance," in *The Science of Social Influence: Advances and Future Progress*, ed. Anthony R. Pratkanis (New York: Psychology Press, 2007), 223.

18. Andrew S. Grove, *Only the Paranoid Survive: How to Exploit the Crisis Points That Challenge Every Company* (New York: Doubleday, 1996), 89.

19. Irving L. Janis, *Groupthink*, 2nd ed. (Boston: Houghton Mifflin, 1982), 268.

20. Gary Katzenstein, "The Debate on Structured Debate: Toward a Unified Theory," *Organizational Behavior and Human Decision Processes* 66 (1996): 316–318.

21. Alexander L. George and Eric K. Stern, "Harnessing Conflict in Foreign Policy Making: From Devil's to Multiple Advocacy," *Presidential Studies Quarterly* 32 (2002): 484, 486.

22. Ibid.

23. Ibid.; Stefan Schulz-Hardt, Marc Jochims, and Dieter Frey, "Productive Conflict in Group Decision Making: Genuine and Contrived Dissent As Strategies to Counteract Biased Information Seeking," *Organizational Behavior and Human Decision Processes* 88 (2002): 563–586.

24. Stefan Schulz-Hardt et al., "Group Decision Making in Hidden Profile Situations: Dissent As a Facilitator for Decision Quality," *Journal of Personality and Social Psychology* 91 (2006): 1080–1093.

25. Brendan Mulvaney, "Red Teams: Strengthening Through Challenge," *Marine Corps Gazette*, July 2012, 63–66; Defense Science Board Task Force, *The Role and Status of DoD Red Teaming Activities* (Washington, DC: 2003), 1–48, www.fas.org/irp/agency/dod/dsb/redteam.pdf.

26. Gene Rowe and George Wright, "The Delphi Technique As a Forecasting Tool: Issues and Analysis," *International Journal of Forecasting* 15 (1999): 353–375.

27. Martin Hilbert, Ian Miles, and Julia Othmer, "Foresight Tools for Participative Policy-Making in Inter-Governmental Processes in Developing Countries: Lessons Learned from the eLAC Policy Priorities Delphi," *Technological Forecasting and Social Change* 76 (2009): 880–896.

28. Gene Row and George Wright, "Expert Opinions in Forecasting: The Role of the Delphi Technique," in *Principles of Forecasting: A Handbook for Researchers and Practitioners*, ed. J. Scott Armstrong (New York: Springer, 2001), 126.

29. Ibid.

30. Ibid., 130; Reid Hastie, "Review Essay: Experimental Evidence on Group Accuracy," in *Information Pooling and Group Decision Making*, ed. Bernard Grofman and Guillermo Owen (Greenwich, CT: JAI Press, 1986), 139.

31. Hastie, "Experimental Evidence on Group Accuracy," 139–145.

32. Ibid., 129.

33. Ibid., 129–130.

34. David H. Gustafson et al., "A Comparative Study of Differences in Subjective Likelihood Estimates Made by Individuals, Interacting Groups, Delphi Groups, and Nominal Groups," *Organizational Behavior and Human Performance* 9 (1973): 280–291.

Chapter 7

1. Donald T. Campbell, "Evolutionary Epistemology," in *The Philosophy of Karl R. Popper*, ed. P. A. Schilpp (LaSalle, IL: Open Court, 1974), 412–463.

2. Leslie Valiant, *Probably Approximately Correct: Nature's Algorithms for Learning and Prospering in a Complex World* (New York: Basic Books, 2013).

3. Tom Kelley and Jonathan Littman, *The Art of Innovation: Lessons in Creativity from IDEO, America's Leading Design Firm* (New York: Doubleday, 2001).

4. Barry Nalebuff and Ian Ayres, *Why Not? How to Use Everyday Ingenuity to Solve Problems Big and Small* (Cambridge, MA: Harvard Business Review Press, 2006).

5. See, for example, Lani Guinier, *The Tyranny of the Majority: Fundamental Fairness in Representative Democracy* (New York: Free Press, 1994); Anthony J. McGann, "The Tyranny of the Supermajority: How Majority Rule Protects Minorities," *Journal of Theoretical Politics* 16 (2004): 53–77.

6. Doug Hall and David Wecker, *Jump Start Your Brain*, 2nd ed. (Cincinnati: Clerisy Press, 2007).

7. Daniel Kahneman and Don Lovallo, "Timid Choices and Bold Forecasts: A Cognitive Perspective on Risk-Taking," *Management Science* 39 (1993): 17–31.

Chapter 8

1. Some affirmative evidence can be found in J. Scott Armstrong, "Combining Forecasts," in *Principles of Forecasting: A Handbook for Researchers and Practitioners*, ed. J. Scott Armstrong (New York: Springer, 2001), 417, 419–420, 427, 433–435.

2. See William P. Bottom, Krishna Ladha, and Gary J. Miller, "Propagation of Individual Bias Through Group Judgment: Error in the Treatment of Asymmetrically Informative Signals," *Journal of Risk and Uncertainty* 25 (2002): 152–154.

3. Francis Galton, "Vox Populi," *Nature* 75 (1907): 450–451.

4. Richard P. Larrick and Jack B. Soll, "Intuitions About Combining Opinions: Misappreciation of the Averaging Principle," *Management Science* 52 (2006): 111–127.

5. See also Clintin P. Davis-Stober, David V. Budescu, Jason Dana, and Stephen B. Broomell, "When Is a Crowd Wise?" *Decision* 2 (2014): 79–101, for a more general mathematical and empirical analysis of the value of diverse estimates.

6. See Scott E. Page, *Diversity and Complexity* (Princeton, NJ: Princeton University Press, 2011), for another mathematical argument for "diversity's inescapable benefits."

7. Bottom, Ladha, and Miller, "Propagation of Individual Bias," 153.

8. Ibid. See also David M. Estlund, *Democratic Authority: A Philosophical Framework* (Princeton, NJ: Princeton University Press, 2008), 225: "The mathematical result is beyond dispute, but it applies only under certain conditions. One is that enough of the votes must be statistically independent. This is often misunderstood. On the overly pessimistic side, many have said this cannot be met since there will always be lots of influence on one another. Few will be independent of each other. What the theorem requires, though, is not causal independence but statistical independence."

9. On some of the technical complexities, see Christian List and Robert E. Goodin, "Epistemic Democracy: Generalizing the Condorcet Jury Theorem," *Journal of Political Philosophy* 9 (2001): 277, 283–288, 295–297.

10. Keith Michael Baker, ed. and trans., *Condorcet: Selected Writings* (Indianapolis: Bobbs-Merrill, 1976), 62. This point is emphasized in Estlund, *Democratic Authority*.

11. Tali Sharot, *The Optimism Bias: A Tour of the Irrationally Positive Brain* (New York: Pantheon Books, 2011).

12. Joseph Henrich et al., "Group Report: What Is the Role of Culture in Bounded Rationality?" in *Bounded Rationality: The Adaptive Toolbox*, ed.

Gerd Gigerenzer and Reinhard Selten (Cambridge, MA: MIT Press, 2001), 353–354, for an entertaining outline in connection with food choices.

13. Baker, *Condorcet*, 56–57.

14. Ibid., 49.

15. Ibid., 61.

Chapter 9

1. Rebecca Greenfield, "The Best and Worst Pundit Predictors of 2012," *The Wire* (blog), November 8, 2012, www.theatlanticwire.com/politics/2012/11/best-and-worst-pundit-predictors-2012/58846/.

2. Philip E. Tetlock, *Expert Political Judgment: How Good Is It? How Can We Know?* (Princeton, NJ: Princeton University Press, 2006).

3. See, for example, James Shanteau, "Competence in Experts: The Role of Task Characteristics," *Organizational Behavior and Human Decision Processes* 53 (1992): 252–266.

4. Nate Silver, *The Signal and the Noise: Why So Many Predictions Fail—But Some Don't* (New York: Penguin, 2012).

5. Greg Sargent, "What Nate Silver Really Accomplished," *The Plum Line* (blog), *Washington Post*, November 21, 2012, www.washingtonpost.com/blogs/plum-line/post/what-nate-silver-really-accomplished/2012/11/21/6f9f10c2-3410-11e2-bfd5-e202b6d7b501_blog.html.

6. Malcolm Gladwell, *Blink: The Power of Thinking Without Thinking* (New York: Little, Brown, 2005), provides many examples of this form of expertise, although few of these examples actually demonstrate true predictive expertise when subjected to scientific scrutiny.

7. Herbert A. Simon and William G. Chase, "Skill in Chess," *American Scientist* 61 (1973): 394–403.

8. Gary Klein, *The Power of Intuition: How to Use Your Gut Feelings to Make Better Decisions at Work* (New York: Doubleday, 2003), provides a popularized account of some examples of case-based expertise.

9. Lee R. Brooks, Geoffrey R. Norman, and Scott W. Allen, "Role of Specific Similarity in a Medical Diagnostic Task," *Journal of Experimental Psychology: General* 120 (1991): 278–287.

10. J. Scott Armstrong, "Combining Forecasts," in *Principles of Forecasting: A Handbook for Researchers and Practitioners*, ed. J. Scott Armstrong (New York: Springer, 2001), 419–420. For many factual questions, of course, a little research would be sufficient to identify the correct answers. But for some factual issues, even significant research is inconclusive, and it is best to consult experts.

11. Ibid., 428.

12. Ibid., 428, 430–431.

13. Ibid., 433.

14. Albert E. Mannes, Jack B. Soll, and Richard P. Larrick, "The Wisdom of Small Crowds," unpublished manuscript, accessed April 2014, http://opim.wharton.upenn.edu/DPlab/papers/workingPapers/Mannes_working_The%20Wisdom%20of%20Small%20Crowds.pdf.

15. Philip Tetlock, "How to Win at Forecasting," *Edge*, December 6, 2012, www.edge.org/conversation/how-to-win-at-forecasting.

Chapter 10

1. Thomas L. Friedman, "When Complexity Is Free," *New York Times*, September 14, 2013, www.nytimes.com/2013/09/15/opinion/sunday/friedman-when-complexity-is-free.html.

2. Kevin J. Boudreau, Nicola Lacetera, and Karim R. Lakhani, "Incentives and Problem Uncertainty in Innovation Contests: An Empirical Analysis," *Management Science* 57 (2011): 843–863.

3. Christian Terwiesch and Yi Xu, "Innovation Contests, Open Innovation, and Multiagent Problem Solving," *Management Science* 54 (2008): 1529–1543.

4. William J. Abernathy and Richard S. Rosenbloom, "Parallel Strategies in Development Projects," *Management Science* 15 (1969): 486–505; Richard R. Nelson and Sidney G. Winter, *An Evolutionary Theory of Economic Change* (Cambridge, MA: Belknap, 1982).

5. Stefan Lindegaard, *The Open Innovation Revolution: Essentials, Roadblocks, and Leadership Skills* (Hoboken, NJ: John Wiley & Sons, 2010); Don Tapscott and Anthony D. Williams, *Wikinomics: How Mass Collaboration Changes Everything* (New York: Penguin, 2006).

6. Jeffrey D. Zients, "Guidance on the Use of Challenges and Prizes to Promote Open Government," Executive Office of the President: Office of Management and Budget, March 8, 2010, www.whitehouse.gov/sites/default/files/omb/assets/memoranda_2010/m10-11.pdf.

7. Ibid.

8. "About Challenge.gov," Challenge.gov, accessed October 4, 2013, https://challenge.gov/p/about.

9. America COMPETES Reauthorization Act of 2010, Pub. L. No. 111-358, 124 Stat. 3982 (2011); Tom Kalil and Tobynn Sturm, "Congress Grants Broad Prize Authority to All Federal Agencies," Open Government

Initiative, December 21, 2010, www.whitehouse.gov/blog/2010/12/21/
congress-grants-broad-prize-authority-all-federal-agencies.

10. Cristin Dorgelo, "Challenge.gov: Two Years and 200 Prizes Later,"
Office of Science and Technology Policy, September 5, 2012, www.white
house.gov/blog/2012/09/05/challengegov-two-years-and-200-prizes-later.

11. For the State Department prize, see Rose Gottemoeller, "Mobiliz-
ing American Ingenuity to Strengthen National Security: A Challenge to
the Public," *DipNote* (US Department of State official blog), August 28,
2013, http://blogs.state.gov/stories/2012/08/28/mobilizing-american-
ingenuity-strengthen-national-security-challenge-public. For the air-
quality prize, see "The My Air, My Health HHS/EPA Challenge," last
modified June 17, 2013, US Environmental Protection Agency, http://epa.
gov/research/challenges/.

12. Office of Science and Technology Policy, *Implementation of Federal
Prize Authority: Progress Report* (Washington, DC: Office of Science and Technology Policy, 2012), 16, www.howto.gov/sites/default/files/implementa-
tion-federal-prize-authority.pdf.

13. Challenge.gov, *Agency Stories: Challenge and Prize Competitions*
(Washington, DC: 2011), 5, www.howto.gov/sites/default/files/agency-
stories-challenge-prize-competitions.pdf.

Chapter 11

1. Friedrich Hayek, "The Use of Knowledge in Society," *American
Economic Review* 35 (1945): 519–530, reprinted in *The Essence of Hayek*, ed.
Chiaki Nishiyama and Kurt R. Leube (Stanford, CA: Hoover Institution,
1984), 211–224. A superb treatment of Hayek's thought is Bruce Caldwell,
Hayek's Challenge: An Intellectual Biography of F. A. Hayek (Chicago: University
of Chicago Press, 2004).

2. Nishiyama and Leube, *The Essence of Hayek*, 212.

3. Ibid., 214.

4. Ibid., 219–220.

5. Ibid., 220.

6. Robert J. Shiller, *Irrational Exuberance*, 2nd ed. (New York: Broadway
Books, 2005).

7. Ibid., 11.

8. Bo Cowgill, "Putting Crowd Wisdom to Work," *Google Official Blog*,
September 21, 2005, http://googleblog.blogspot.com/2005/09/putting-
crowd-wisdom-to-work.html.

9. Justin Wolfers and Eric Zitzewitz, "Prediction Markets," *Journal of Economic Perspectives* 18 (2004): 107–126.

10. Saul Levmore, "Simply Efficient Markets and the Role of Regulation: Lessons from the Iowa Electronic Markets and the Hollywood Stock Exchange," *Journal of Corporation Law* 28 (2003): 593.

11. Emile Servan-Schreiber et al., "Prediction Markets: Does Money Matter?" *Electronic Markets* 14 (2004): 243–251.

12. Richard Roll, "Orange Juice and Weather," *American Economic Review* 74 (1984): 871.

13. See Wolfers and Zitzewitz, "Prediction Markets," 113–114.

14. Donald N. Thompson, *Oracles: How Prediction Markets Turn Employees into Visionaries* (Boston: Harvard Business Review Press, 2012), 105.

15. Ibid., 103.

16. Ibid., 105.

17. Kay-Yut Chen and Charles R. Plott, "Information Aggregation Mechanisms: Concept, Design, and Implementation for a Sales Forecasting Problem," working paper, Social Science, Division of the Humanities and Social Sciences, California Institute of Technology, March 2002, 3, http://authors.library.caltech.edu/44358/1/wp1131.pdf (describing variation of this model employed by Hewlett-Packard).

18. Wolfers & Zitzewitz, "Prediction Markets," 112; Robert W. Hahn & Paul C. Tetlock, "Harnessing the Power of Information: A New Approach to Economic Development," working paper, AEI-Brookings Joint Center for Regulatory Studies, 2004, 4, http://papers.ssrn.com/sol3/papers.cfm?abstract_id=641444.

19. Wolfers and Zitzewitz, "Prediction Markets," 112.

20. Thompson, *Oracles*, 50.

21. For the IEM results, see "They All Got It Right: Polls, Markets, and Models," *PBS NewsHour*, November 7, 2012, www.pbs.org/newshour/businessdesk/2012/11/they-all-got-it-right-polls-ma.html. For the final tally, see "2012 Presidential Election Results," *Washington Post*, November 19, 2012, www.washingtonpost.com/wp-srv/special/politics/election-map-2012/president/.

22. Joyce Berg et al., "Results from a Dozen Years of Election Futures Market Research," unpublished manuscript, March 2003, http://tippie.uiowa.edu/iem/research/papers/bergforsythenelsonrietz_2008.pdf; Joyce E. Berg and Thomas A. Rietz, "Prediction Markets as Decision Support Systems," *Information Systems Frontiers* 5 (2003): 79–93.

23. Donald Granberg and Edward Brent, "When Prophecy Bends: The Preference-Expectation Link in U.S. Presidential Elections, 1952–1980," *Journal of Personality and Social Psychology* 45 (1983): 479.

24. Koleman S. Strumpf, *Manipulating the Iowa Political Stock Market*, unpublished manuscript, 2004, cited in Wolfers and Zitzewitz, "Prediction Markets," 118.

25. Robert Forsythe, Thomas A. Rietz, and Thomas W. Ross, "Wishes, Expectations and Actions: A Survey on Price Formation in Election Stock Markets," *Journal of Economic Behavior and Organization* 39 (1999): 94.

26. Ibid., 94–95.

27. Charles G. Lord, Lee Ross, and Mark R. Lepper, "Biased Assimilation and Attitude Polarization: The Effects of Prior Theories on Subsequently Considered Evidence," *Journal of Personality and Social Psychology* 37 (1979): 2098–2109. See also Muzafer Sherif and Carl I. Hovland, *Social Judgment: Assimilation and Contrast Effects in Communication and Attitude Change* (New Haven, CT: Yale University Press, 1961), 188 (discussing how individuals filter information to conform to their preexisting positions).

28. Forsythe, Rietz, and Ross, "Wishes," 94.

29. Berg et al., *Election Futures Market Research*, 42.

30. Forsythe, Rietz, and Ross, "Wishes," 99–100. The term "quasirational" comes from Richard H. Thaler, *Quasi-Rational Economics* (New York: Russell Sage Foundation, 1991), xxi.

31. Richard H. Thaler and William T. Ziemba, "Anomalies: Parimutuel Betting Markets: Racetracks and Lotteries," *Journal of Economic Perspectives* 2 (1988): 163, explores favorite-longshot bias. See also Charles F. Manski, "Interpreting the Predictions of Prediction Markets," unpublished manuscript, August 2005, www.aeaweb.org/assa/2006/0106_1015_0703.pdf, which summarizes horse-race data findings.

32. David Forrest and Ian McHale, "Longshot Bias: Insights from the Betting Market on Men's Tennis," in *Information Efficiency in Financial and Betting Markets*, ed. Leighton Vaughan Williams (Cambridge: Cambridge University Press, 2005), 215–230.

33. Interestingly, some sports betting shows the opposite pattern; in English professional football, long shots have been found to be underpriced. See David Forrest and Robert Simmons, "Efficiency of the Odds on English Professional Football Matches," in *Information Efficiency*, ed. Williams, 336.

34. The most important evidence can be found on Tradesports's predictions, where highly unlikely outcomes were overpriced in a number of domains. See Wolfers and Zitzewitz, "Prediction Markets," 117.

35. See Richard H. Thaler, ed., *Advances in Behavioral Finance*, vol. 2 (Princeton, NJ: Princeton University Press, 2009); and see Kay-Yut Chen, Leslie R. Fine, and Bernardo A. Huberman, "Eliminating Public Knowledge Biases in Information-Aggregation Markets," *Management Science* 50 (2004): 983–994, for one example of a method of correcting prediction market

outputs for risk-attitudes and shared-information biases, increasing accuracy over the raw market prices.

36. Shiller, *Irrational Exuberance*, 2.

37. For much evidence, see Thaler, *Advances in Behavioral Finance*.

38. Erin Jordan, "Iowa Electronic Markets Yields Near-Accurate Result," *Des Moines Register*, November 10, 2004.

Chapter 12

1. Meredith Halama, "NAI Seeking Public Comment on Revised Code of Conduct," *Network Advertising Initiative*, March 1, 2013, www.networkad vertising.org/blog/nai-seeking-public-comment-revised-code-of-conduct.

2. Laura Carroll, "Opinions Please! Retailers Seeking Public's Input," *Las Vegas Review-Journal*, July 1, 2013, www.reviewjournal.com/business/ retail/opinions-please-retailers-seeking-publics-input.

3. Ibid.

4. Korri Kezar, "Austin Gun Manufacturer Seeking Public Input," *Community Impact Newspaper*, June 25, 2013, http://impactnews.com/austin-metro/round-rock-pflugerville-hutto/gun-manufacturer-seeking-public-input/; "The Crowdsourced Smart Rifle," *TrackingPoint*, June 21, 2013, https://tracking-point.com/labs/future/.

Chapter 13

1. D. J. Devine and J. L. Phillips, "Do Smart Teams Do Better: A Meta-analysis of Cognitive Ability and Team Performance," *Small Group Research* 32 (2001): 507–532; Suzanne T. Bell, "Deep-Level Composition Variables as Predictors of Team Performance: A Meta-analysis," *Journal of Applied Psychology* 92 (2007): 595–615.

2. Walter Mischel, *Personality and Assessment* (New York: Wiley, 1968).

3. Lee Ross and Richard E. Nisbett, *The Person and the Situation: Perspectives of Social Psychology* (New York: McGraw-Hill, 1991).

4. Malcolm Gladwell, "Personality Plus," *New Yorker*, September 2004, 42.

5. See, for example, Kenneth M. Nowack, "Is the Myers Briggs Type Indicator the Right Tool to Use?" *Performance in Practice, American Society of Training and Development* (Fall 1996): 6.

6. Christina A. Rideout and Susan A. Richardson, "A Teambuilding Model: Appreciating Differences Using the Myers-Briggs Type Indicator with Developmental Theory," *Journal of Counseling and Development*, 67 (1989): 532. Tricia Varvel et al., "Team Effectiveness and Individual Myers-Briggs

Personality Dimensions," *Journal of Management in Engineering* 20 (2004): 146, have similar findings: "This research did not conclude that a particular combination of personality type preferences have a direct incidence on team effectiveness."

7. Bell, "Deep-Level Composition Variables," 595; Steve W. J. Kozlowski and Bradford S. Bell, "Work Groups and Teams in Organizations," in *Handbook of Psychology: Industrial and Organizational Psychology*, 2nd ed., ed. Randy K. Otto (New York: Wiley, 2013), 12:412.

8. Ibid.

9. Anita Woolley et al., "Evidence for a Collective Intelligence Factor in the Performance of Human Groups," *Science* 330 (2010): 686–688.

10. Simon Baron-Cohen et al., "The 'Reading the Mind in the Eyes' Test, Revised Version: A Study with Normal Adults, and Adults with Asperger Syndrome or High-Functioning Autism," *Journal of Child Psychology and Psychiatry* 42 (2001): 241–251.

11. Anita W. Woolley and Thomas W. Malone, "What Makes a Team Smarter? More Women," *Harvard Business Review*, June 2011, http://hbr.org/2011/06/defend-your-research-what-makes-a-team-smarter-more-women/.

12. Linus Torvalds and David Diamond, *Just for Fun: The Story of an Accidental Revolutionary* (New York: HarperCollins, 2001).

13. Andrew Lih, *The Wikipedia Revolution: How a Bunch of Nobodies Created the World's Greatest Encyclopedia* (New York: Hyperion, 2009).

Index

Acknowledgments

This short book has been very long in coming. We decided to write it in 2007, after several collaborative endeavors involving deliberation by citizens and jurors. In 2009, however, Sunstein joined the Obama administration, and the project was put on hold until 2012, when we began again. As the text suggests, the book has been informed by Sunstein's experience and by a sense of what goes well, and what goes a bit less well, in government.

We are grateful to our superb editor, Jeff Kehoe, both for his patience and for providing excellent guidance, especially at crucial moments. Three anonymous reviewers provided terrific comments and general inspiration. Sunstein gives particular thanks to his wife, Samantha Power, for many discussions of these questions, and Hastie thanks Nancy Pennington for always having the best ideas. Daniel Kanter provided superb research assistance and excellent comments.

Both of us have done a great deal of work on this topic, and this book draws heavily from some of that work, above all, Cass R. Sunstein and Reid Hastie, "Garbage In, Garbage Out? Some Micro Sources of Macro Errors," *Journal of Institutional Economics* (2014), and Cass R. Sunstein, "Group Judgments," *New York University Law Review* 80 (2005): 962–1049. Much of the latter article appears in Cass R. Sunstein, *Infotopia: How Many Minds Produce Knowledge* (New York: Oxford University Press, 2006). We are grateful to the editors of the *Journal of Institutional Economics* and the *New York*

University Law Review for permission to draw from that material here. We have also drawn on Daniel Gigone and Reid Hastie, "Proper Analysis of the Accuracy of Group Judgment," *Psychological Bulletin* 121 (1997): 149, 161–162; and Reid Hastie, "Review Essay: Experimental Evidence on Group Accuracy," in *Information Pooling and Group Decision Making*, ed. Bernard Grofman and Guillermo Owen (Greenwich, CT: JAI Press, 1986), 129–158. Readers who are interested in more technical presentations might consult that work.

About the Authors

Cass R. Sunstein is the Robert Walmsley University Professor at Harvard University. He is the founder and director of the Program on Behavioral Economics and Public Policy at Harvard Law School. From 2009 to 2012 he served as Administrator of the White House Office of Information and Regulatory Affairs, and from 2013 to 2014 he served on the President's Review Group on Intelligence and Communications Technologies. He has worked with a number of nations as well as private firms on applications of behavioral economics. His many books include *Simpler: The Future of Government* and *Nudge: Improving Decisions About Health, Wealth, and Happiness* (with Richard H. Thaler).

Reid Hastie is an expert on the psychology of decision making, especially by groups. He has authored or coauthored several academic books, including *Rational Choice in an Uncertain World*. He is currently the Ralph and Dorothy Keller Distinguished Service Professor of Behavioral Science at the University of Chicago Booth School of Business.